Caribbean Cruising

Your Guide to the Perfect Sailing Holiday

Jane and John Gibb

With an Introduction by John Kretschmer

S

Sheridan House

This edition first published 2003
by Sheridan House Inc.
145 Palisade Street
Dobbs Ferry, New York 10522
www.sheridanhouse.com

First published 2002 in the United Kindgom
by Adlard Coles Nautical

Photographs by John Gibb; illustrations by Jane Gibb

The publisher takes no responsibility for the use of any of the materials or
methods described in the book, or for the products thereof.

Library of Congress Cataloging-in-Publication Data

Gibb, Jane.
    Caribbean cruising : your guide to the perfect sailing holiday / Jane
  Gibb and John Gibb, with introduction by John Kretschmer ;
  photographs by John Gibb ; illustrations by Jane Gibb.
        p. cm
    Includes bibliographical references and index.
    ISBN 1-57409-172-7
    1. Yachting–Caribbean Area–Guidebooks.
    2. Caribbean Area–Guidebooks. I. Gibb, John. II. Title.
    GV817.C37 G53 2003
    797. 1'246'09729–dc22   20003009880

With an introduction and edited by John Kretschmer
Managing editor: Janine Simon

Printed in China
ISBN 1-57409-172-7

Contents

Introduction

The Caribbean taunts North American sailors. Arguably the world's finest cruising ground, the islands of the Antilles, lie tantalizingly over the horizon, a mere 1,000–1,500 miles away. If you can con your boat along at six knots, that translates into around ten days at sea before you and your crew fetch up in paradise.

Unfortunately it is not that easy. While European sailors face the not unpleasant prospect of a long but leisurely stroll across the Atlantic, running before the so-called "ladies' trades," American and Canadian sailors must prepare for a shorter but in many ways more challenging passage. Author and circumnavigator Jimmy Cornell offers this cautious advice in his popular book, *World Cruising Routes*, "The most direct route (from the USA to the Virgin Islands) leads well offshore and should only be attempted with a thoroughly tested boat and crew. The timing for the passage is critical."

More often than not, the passage south and east to the islands from almost anywhere along the East Coast is a bash, and we are not talking about a party with steel drums and rum punch, that comes after landfall. We're talking about a seven- to twelve-day passage slugging it out against the prevailing winds and currents, and that is without the bad luck of encountering a gale.

I have sailed between the East Coast, be it New England, New York, the Chesapeake Bay, the Carolinas or Florida and the Caribbean islands dozens of times. While departure can be made from several different points, as Jimmy Cornell observes, the timing for a safe weather window is somewhat limited.

Timing

The best time to start for the islands is from late October through late November. This is usually a period of settled weather near the end of the hurricane season but before the advent of continental gales and nasty nor'easters. This timing also places you in the islands early in the season, allowing for seven or eight months of carefree cruising before contemplating a return passage or the need to find refuge in Trinidad or Venezuela for a looming hurricane season.

If you are sailing the direct offshore route, make sure that there are not any late season tropical low-pressure systems brewing. In addition to NOAA and private weather routing services, The Weather Channel and other general media outlets are obsessed with hurricanes, tracking and broadcasting every dip in barometric pressure. Finding particulars about the tropical weather is not difficult. With a clear tropical weather forecast, many sailors opt to push off the coast on the leading edge of a cold front, taking advantage of the strong but favorable west and northwest winds to gain easting before the wind clocks and the prevailing easterlies that predominate over the route are encountered.

Long-range weather forecasts are better than ever and sailors heading offshore to the Caribbean should avail themselves of these excellent services. However, they must also be prepared for the forecast to be inaccurate, and be ready to slug their way south.

The route

Departure points for Caribbean passages fall into three geographic regions: New England, Mid-Atlantic, and Florida. Generally speaking, the further north your departure, the less windward sailing will be encountered. The U.S./Canadian coast bends dramatically east once north of New York, making the route to the Caribbean more southerly. Winds from the southern quadrant are rare in the fall. If you time your passage with a passing cold front you can often ride a cool westerly several hundred miles offshore. Keep in mind, however, that as the wind clocks to the northeast, il will stir up the Gulf Stream current, which varies in width from fifty to one hundred miles. Make all speed to cross the infamous Gulf Stream before the wind is in opposition and life aboard become lumpy and uncomfortable.

The prevailing easterlies usually kick in just below the thirtieth parallel. If you have departed on the edge of a cold front from Newport, Rhode Island, for example, by the time you encounter the easterlies, you should be in a position to close reach down to the islands. Of course, the further north your departure point the greater the likelihood you'll be exposed to bitter cold weather. Conversely, if you leave from too far south, say below Charleston, South Carolina, the odds of beating your way to the islands are much greater. The geography of the East Coast is deceptive. From any point below the Carolinas, you'll spend more time sailing east than south in pursuit of the islands.

Steve Black, founder of the popular West Marine Caribbean 1500 Cruising Rally, has chosen the mouth of the Chesapeake Bay as the ideal staging point for the passage to Tortola in the British Virgin Islands. I tend to agree with him. This route usually avoids the biting arctic winds that can strike New England and the Canadian Maritime Provinces in the late fall. It also gives you a full day to find your sea legs before meeting the Gulf Stream. Although the rally begins north of Cape Hatteras, frequent westerlies near the coast usually escort you offshore quickly, diminishing the impact of the unpredictable weather that haunt this low slung, windswept headland.

Black does not downplay the serious nature of the passage. "Every year we have some excitement," he explains, "preparation is the key. The crew and the boat have to be ready for extreme weather." Like with the popular ARC Rally across the Atlantic, many North American sailors use the Caribbean 1500, which departs in early November, as a focus point for planning their passage to the islands. 2002 was the 12th running of the event and more than fifty boats participated.

If you simply dread the idea of an offshore passage of any length, there is another route to the islands. Despite the fact that it is almost always a windward slog, more boats depart from Central and South Florida than any other point along the coast. Coined "the thorny path," this route makes use of well-placed islands, like stepping stones, allowing cautious and patient cruisers the opportunity to day sail nearly all the way south. By riding each passing cold front a little further east and south, and patiently waiting in safe anchorages until the easterlies blow themselves out before the next front, it is possible to reach the islands without the need for night watches.

John Kretschmer

1

Getting There

For those of us who sail, cruising the islands of the Caribbean has always conjured visions of gliding over warm crystal waters into idyllic palm fringed anchorages under limitless blue skies dotted with those adorable cotton ball clouds.

When HONEY JAR brought us safely across the Atlantic from England we cruised the Caribbean for the next 10 years. At the end of each season, we left the area and spent most of our summers exploring the East Coast and the Canadian Maritimes; it was a love affair that still endures. As fall approached we'd drag ourselves away from the fascinations of New England and head south with the other Snowbirds, dipping in and out of our favorite ports and harbors along the way. Short of mailing the boat, we've tried most routes both ways.

As outlined in John Kretschmer's introduction there are many routes for the North American sailor to get his boat to the sun, and just getting to the starting point can be part of the fun. Our first stop on leaving Maine was Newport, Rhode Island. When we tired of watching boats preparing for serious passage making we'd while away hours in Armchair Sailor Bookstore (now Bluewater Books) browsing their vast selection of marine books and charts.

Further south, conning the boat down the East River and into New York at dawn proved an unforgettable experience with the Chrysler building (my personal favorite) glowing in the early sunlight. A mooring at the 79th Street Yacht Basin was very convenient for sightseeing but we found staying in Great Kills, further south, a quieter anchorage the next time and took the Staten Island ferry for the Big Apple.

The Chesapeake Bay was usually our next stop. Once we'd sailed past the big green lady it seemed to take forever trailing down New Jersey, clawing

Photo opposite: Pelicans fish for breakfast as the anchorage wakes to another sunny day. By sunset the boats will have come and gone but the pelicans will still be there tomorrow.

around the Cape May shoals and plowing endlessly up the Delaware, keeping well out of the way of huge container traffic. Turning into the sanctuary of the Chesapeake and Delaware Canal brought us into the Chesapeake to recapture the last of the milder weather. This is a popular area for southbound boats gathering in the fall and we timed our arrivals to include the Annapolis Boat Show in early October. The anchorages soon fill with boats as friends rendezvous and shop for last purchases. Many boats leave from Norfolk, Virginia for a direct passage to the Caribbean but some slip down behind Hatteras via the Intracoastal Waterway to Beaufort, North Carolina, another popular gathering spot. Both have their merits as we know.

The ICW is an easy way to go south, or north, for those not wanting to make a sea passage and the views are stunning. As you only travel by day it takes time but cruising is about taking it easy and we always found interesting places to stop. Sometimes out in the wild with only the water birds for company; other times staying for days in busy towns visiting museums to brush up on our history.

Weather forecasts are seldom accurate for more than seventy two hours, as we found out. Three days out from Beaufort, North Carolina, we were becalmed with only faint southerly winds. Tacking back and forth brought little progress except to the east. Next stop Africa? The following year the tables were turned. Hurricane Mitch had blown himself to the Yucatán and

Provisioning

In 20 years of cruising (the last 10 continuous) I have never bothered to varnish cans or to remove labels. I do mark the tops with the contents and best by date so that when viewed from above they can be identified easily.

Storing flour, rice, pasta and the like in tightly sealed plastic containers, with a few bay leaves, is good for keeping weevils and other livestock away. Citrus fruits, apples, pears and pineapples keep well, but large bunches of bananas tend to ripen all at once. To prevent avocados from rotting before ripening keep them away from citrus fruit. Soft fruits tend to rot quickly so eat them first. Root vegetables, with the exception of carrots, keep well in a cool locker. Look them over every two days and rub off any sprouting eyes. Carrots go slimy and smell foul if not kept in the refrigerator. Butternut squash keeps very well for weeks but life for zucchini and cucumber is limited outside the refrigerator. Green cabbage keeps well but lettuce will only last a couple of days except for the iceberg variety; peel both leaf by leaf, and keep in a cool place.

we judged it safe to leave Norfolk, Virginia. Three days out and Mitch did a U turn heading back to Florida and forecast bound for Bermuda. There was no turning back for us. For nine days we headed south east under storm rig with 50 knots, even within sight of St. Martin. You just never know.

Then there's Bermuda. It sits like a little jewel in the Atlantic and is an excellent staging post to the sun and is top of our favorite stopovers. Surprisingly, it is almost equidistant from most of the East Coat, making it a convenient place to break the journey into two more manageable bites. Six

To make a basic calculation for enough stores for the trip: count mouths to feed x meals per day x days of passage and double the total for safety.

Water

Water consumption will have to be monitored on passage unless you have a water-maker, but don't cut down on drinking water rations. Most people don't drink enough water even in our temperate climate but it is vital to drink sufficient water as the weather gets hotter, for dehydration is insidious (See chapter 17).

Apart from bottled water in the emergency bag, it is wise to carry extra water wherever it can be stowed, even on deck, in case the main tank gets contaminated. Watermakers can fail, so it is a mistake to think that minimal tankage is required if you have one installed. Make sure your tanks are very clean.

Baking bread is not difficult using dried yeast and bread flour. If that sounds too tricky try sourdough recipes that don't require yeast nor proving but get some practice in before leaving to find a recipe that suits all aboard.

Canned food will probably play a part in the passage diet. The quality of canned food today means tasty meals are almost guaranteed and even the most artless crew can produce a decent meal when pointed at a selection of cans, an opener and the galley stove. On a long passage, taking short cuts—using part-prepared, freeze-dried, or canned products—is not considered cheating.

to seven days will get you there from most places and you can rest up and enjoy the many delights of the islands for days or weeks while you wait for the best conditions and your final slide to the sun.

Another of our favorites was St. Augustine, Florida where one time we spent weeks refitting in a friendly little boat yard.

Leaving Florida for the Bahamas makes you feel you're really on your way; the heat, startling colors and the crystal water. In Georgetown it was difficult to tear ourselves away from the thriving community of gregarious cruisers in this well protected harbor.

For how to make the most comfortable progress further east in day hops along the Spanish Virgins read *The Gentleman's Guide to Passages South* by Bruce Van Sant. Written with humor and stuffed full of pertinent advice on working the weather fronts for easy easting, the book shows you how to take the sting out of the Thorny Path.

See you in the Caribbean!

2

The Caribbean

The West Indies is the archipelago dividing the Caribbean Sea and the Atlantic Ocean. This includes the Bahamas, the Greater Antilles (Cuba, Jamaica, Haiti, the Dominican Republic and Puerto Rico), the Lesser Antilles from the Virgin Islands to Trinidad and Tobago, including Barbados and the islands on the North coast of Venezuela (Aruba, Bonaire and Curaçao).

The term Antilles applies to all the islands in the West Indies, excluding the Bahamas. The Caribbean covers the total area of the Caribbean Sea from the Lesser Antilles in the east to the Panamanian peninsula in the west. In this book the term Caribbean is used to denote the popular area of smaller islands at the eastern end of the Caribbean Sea, frequently enjoyed by cruising and charter boats and other vacationers. This group of islands is comprised of the Leeward and Windward Islands in the Lesser Antilles, also Barbados as well as Trinidad and Tobago.

Even though they lie so close together, the islands have developed their own special character and each one is worth a visit. The common factor shared by all the islands is the tropical climate: a perpetual heat wave, with abundant rain showers on most of the islands, periodic strong winds and a hurricane season. But it is the hot sun, the swaying palms over white sands, the warm turquoise seas and the constant breezes that bring the tourist and the cruiser.

The Leeward Islands run in an arc from the Virgin Islands down to, and including, Dominica. Between these islands the arc splits in two: on the outer, Atlantic side the islands of Anegada, Anguilla, Barbuda, Antigua and the eastern half of Guadeloupe are low-lying, being formed mainly of coral and limestone. Because of this, they tend to have less rainfall and are arid. The islands on the inside, in the Caribbean Sea, are Saba, Statia, St. Kitts, Montserrat and the western half of Guadeloupe. These green and fertile islands are all that remain of the top end of a chain of volcanoes and mountain peaks lying along the edge of one of the world's shifting plates between the Atlantic Ocean and the Caribbean Sea.

The Windward Islands (from Martinique southwards) being a continuation of the volcanic chain are mountainous, attracting rain and, as a result, have lush vegetation–many with rainforests.

U.S. Virgin Islands

The U.S. Virgin Islands are "Little America" in the tropics. The US dollar and the English language prevail, together with the fast food chains, making these islands, which require no formalities for entry by US citizens, big favorites.

The three main islands are St. Thomas, St. John and, 35 miles to the south, St. Croix (pronounced St. Croy); there are, additionally, several

smaller islands. The USVIs were owned by the Danes until bought by the United States in 1917 and still show evidence of their Danish history in some of the buildings and the street names in the capital, Charlotte Amalie on St. Thomas. This large natural harbor is a busy commercial port with, most days, several huge cruise liners lying bow to stern along the dock. This is a useful anchorage for shopping and you can enjoy a trip up in the cable car to take in the view. Next door, in Crown Bay, you'll find quieter and cleaner conditions and the town is reached easily by dinghy. St. Thomas has good service yards but few pleasant anchorages.

Nearly all of St. John, plus the surrounding seabed, is a

Throughout the islands, colonial influences show in the many well-preserved buildings. Tall windows, intricate ironwork and shaded balconies speak of a by-gone age.

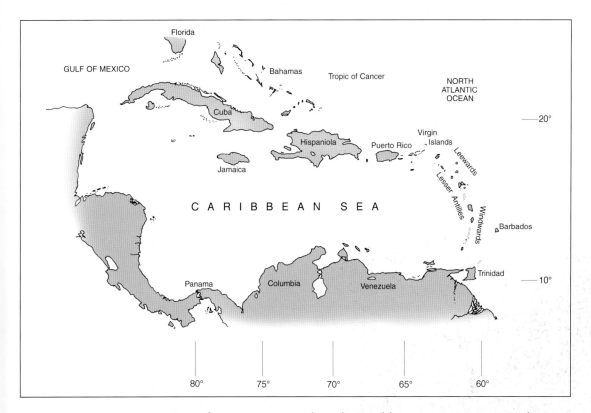

From east to west, say from Antigua to Belize, the Caribbean Sea is approximately 1500 miles wide. Surprisingly, the Panama canal is east of Florida.

National Park with restrictions on development, making it one of the islands least spoiled by tourism. The National Park Office is on the dock in Cruz Bay where you can pick up useful information about the rules concerning boats using the Park. The Park Service has laid down over 200 moorings in many of the bays and anchoring is forbidden in some parts. Coral Bay, on the south east, is not a tourist attraction and is quiet; it is a favorite with many of the more charismatic and exotic long-term cruisers, who display ingenuity and artistic talents in their craft.

St. Croix has a particularly strong Danish flavor. It's a good day's sail (about 35 miles south), so you'll need to set off at the crack of dawn to make Christiansted in daylight. But the effort is worth it to admire the historic buildings on this island, away from the crowds.

British Virgin Islands

From the Virgin Islands to Trinidad, the string of islands that separate the Atlantic Ocean and Caribbean Sea enticed the early explorers. The islands hold the same allure today.

This group of tiny islands has been a favorite with seafarers from the time the first settlers paddled their primitive crafts up from South America, long before Columbus arrived in 1493. The islands languished in the sun until Britain acquired them in 1666 when they developed a taste for piracy. Blackbeard and Captain Morgan, among others, favored the islands and shivered the timbers of their victims. Even Sir Francis Drake is considered "just another pirate" here, though he gave his name to the channel that provides some of the best cruising in the Caribbean.

There are (apart from 10 or so rocky outcrops that don't qualify) about 36 islands in the group, with about half being inhabited. These three dozen islands give a range of places to anchor, bask, picnic, shop, eat, drink, snorkel and cruise around—enough to please the most picky of gunkholers. Although the islands are popular with charter companies, there are still plenty of quiet anchorages little used by their boats.

Everywhere the view is of green islands with sloping hills, palm-edged bays and beaches whose color can be blinding white, through pale cream to soft pink and beige. Jewel-like colors are reflected in the sea: lapis blue, turquoise, emerald and gold. Countless anchorages offer interesting rocks and exotic fish, plants and birds. The sailing is fun but if conditions get iffy, it's seldom more than an hour to reach somewhere comfortable.

The charts show two parallel island strings separated by the three-mile wide Sir Francis Drake Channel. Twenty miles long, and lying roughly due

The Pitons, St Lucia: once seen, never forgotten. The town of Souffrière sits between the twin peaks.

east/west, this channel provides arguably some of the most delightful, and certainly the easiest, cruising in the Caribbean. After breakfast (not too early), you can leave the pretty place you chose last night and tack easily across to the next little stunner on the other side and pick the best spot before others arrive. After lunch, spend the afternoon snorkeling or strolling ashore before returning in time for sundowners with your neighboring cruisers and think about doing it all over again tomorrow.

Cruising the Virgin Islands is one place where your lightweight sail can get an airing: having sailed up to Virgin Gorda at the eastern end, you have the delightful prospect of sliding all the way down the Sir Frances Drake Passage on a run. The Virgins are more affected by the weather systems coming off the U.S. East Coast, giving variable conditions which you can use to your advantage when making passages eastward.

Sint Maarten/St. Martin

The island is half Dutch and half French but there are no restrictions on traveling from one side to the other. The large lagoon on the western end is a very busy spot. Stay long enough in Simpson Bay Lagoon and you'll see just about every cruiser in the Caribbean. So what's the draw? Abundant marine

Yachts gather in St Martin's lagoon to enjoy the many facilities which include marine services, French food and a vibrant social life.

services is one answer, and duty free goods is another; if you're looking for electronics, this is *the* place. French-speaking St. Martin is under the jurisdiction of Guadeloupe. The island hosts the Heineken Regatta, one of the most popular events in the cruising calendar. Don't get stuck in the lagoon; you'll find that the bays on the French side are quieter and less crowded.

Anguilla

Little more than four miles off the north coast of St. Martin, Anguilla is a country in its own right and, staunchly proud of its British heritage, it was very upset when it was summarily lumped together with St. Kitts for administrative purposes in 1967. After a short Gilbert and Sullivan-style rebellion, with shots fired but no fatalities, Anguilla was returned to British rule and ruffled feathers were smoothed. The island is now a peaceful retreat for tourists, cruisers and a large colony of exquisite long-tailed tropic birds.

St. Barthélemy aka St. Barts

St. Barts (measuring only five miles by three) is very French, very chic and very expensive but utterly charming. Until recently, it was the haunt of only the rich and famous who wanted to get away from it all. Before them, pirates favored St. Barts as a hide-away and their treasure is rumored to still be buried somewhere on this island. It's worth a visit to study the luxury yachts hanging off the dock in Gustavia together with the luxury goods in the shops; plus you can enjoy a walk to nearby Anse Galet, a shell beach. St. Barts also falls under Guadeloupe's jurisdiction and the language is French.

The Volcanic Islands

Running parallel, but a little to the west of the main chain, are five small volcanic islands that seem to spring out of the sea to touch heaven. With their heads in the clouds, these steep islands catch plenty of rain, keeping them richly green. Being offset from the main chain, the islands remain delightfully unspoiled but, with only a handful of safe anchorages, you need to watch the weather if you want to make the trip ashore.

Saba
Lying to the northwest, Saba, barely two miles wide, rises like a cone from the ocean to a peak of 3000 feet. Steep-to shores have kept this fairy-tale island largely unsullied by commercialism. A tribute to their Dutch heritage, the two gingerbread towns are pin-neat and the population industrious, building against impossible odds their own tiny airstrip. Famed for its exclusive handmade lace and spectacular undersea cliff diving, Saba is perhaps best visited by ferry, diveboat or flight for there are no safe anchorages.

St. Eustatius
More usually known as Statia, St. Eustatius is a peaceful, dreamy island with a group of small mountains at the north end while at its southern end, an extinct volcano rises almost 2000 feet, cupping a rain forest in its crater. In between, the land rolls gently over green hills. Two hundred years ago, this little haven of tranquillity was the trading center of the West Indies and was dubbed the Golden Rock. Nowadays the island is a serene retreat from modern day

bustle. In the well preserved colonial house, now a museum, read a page from the diary of an intrepid 18th-century English lady traveler who commented pithily on the lazy people who "sat around and smoked all day."

St. Kitts

St. Kitts forms a two-island state with Nevis, having been claimed for the crown by Thomas Warner in 1624; they formed the first English settlement in the Leewards. By the 1770s, St. Kitts was the richest colony in the British Empire, as witnessed by many fine plantation houses, set in the cool of the mountain slopes and now run as hotels.

Nevis

Lying like the dot to St. Kitts exclamation mark, Nevis sits only two miles from her big sister but the 5- by 6-mile island talks periodically of independence; this would make her one of the smallest nations in the world. Like her sibling, she sports a central extinct volcano surrounded by low fertiles slopes running to the shore. But perhaps the island's lasting fame is as the location for the marriage of Horatio Nelson to Frances Nisbet in 1787.

Redonda

Barely a mile wide, Redonda rises to an amazing 1000 feet. Hardly more than rock, with some scrubby cactus, this tiny island has a history that reads like something out of a comic opera. Claimed by the British in 1865 for the phosphates that were discovered there, the mines thrived for about 50 years under considerable challenges, not the least being the transport between peak and beach of all the mined minerals and personnel via a water-weighted cable car. Running alongside this enterprise was Matthew Shiel, of Irish decent, who decided, with the aid of a handy bishop, to crown his only son King Filipe I of Redonda. Royal duties being somewhat lean in such a small kingdom, Shiel Jr returned to England to become a novelist, admired by no lesser a personage than H.G. Wells. After his death, Shiel's heritage passed through a succession of friends. The current incumbent did little more than plant a flag on the summit before returning home to England.

Montserrat

Montserrat is the southern-most of the inside group of Leeward islands. Despite its small size (5 x 9 miles), it still manages to put up a 3000-feet volcano that is visibly active. For centuries the volcano was thought to be a dead giant, but the giant was only sleeping and in 1995 his troubled awakening caused most of the population to shift away from the south. Later eruptions devastated Plymouth, the capital, the only airstrip and thus, the economy. Until then, the production of Sea Island Cotton and a relaxed style of tourism had provided most of the prosperity; ironically, it was the island's famed tranquillity that had attracted the quiet-seeking tourists. The volcano is still very active and it is recommended to pass at least 3 to 5 miles to the east and more than 15 miles to the west to avoid the damage from hot ash. Check local conditions before anchoring in the northern bays as access is sometimes forbidden.

Antigua and Barbuda

Antigua was the home port in the West Indies for Admiral Nelson and his fleet in 1784 and Britain's most important base in the West Indies at that time. The dockyard, still bearing his name, is as active as in Nelson's day and has not changed a lot. Nearly all the original, attractive buildings are well preserved and in use, some with marine services and others for tourism such as the Copper and Lumber Store, now a charming hotel.

Falmouth Harbour, around the corner westward, is where the big boys play. Anchor along the southeastern shore to watch the comings and goings during Antigua Race Week and monitor Montserrat's volcano from a safe distance. The island is rather flat and subject to drought (unusual in the Caribbean) but boasts 365 beaches and is worth exploring away from the most popular spots.

Barbuda, just over 20 miles to the north, is bound by numerous reefs and rises to little more than 100 feet.

Guadeloupe

Guadeloupe is shaped like a butterfly and gathers under her wings the islands of Marie-Galante and the charming little Iles des Saintes. Since Guadeloupe is a department of France, the economy is well supported from the mainland and this is reflected in the restaurants. The language is French. A shallow river channel divides the two "wings" and can be traversed to open water on both sides but the road bridge openings should be checked for timing. Guadeloupe also has a unique madras woven cotton fabric that is traditional to the island, well worth buying.

By themselves, Iles des Saintes are like fairy islands and one could spend some time among them and not be bored. Guadeloupe is also the finish line for the Route du Rhum.

Dominica

This island may be small but makes up for it with its mountains, some of the tallest in the islands. It's almost as if the island has been squeezed to form tall peaks and steep valleys. Rain clouds compete with each other to dump the most showers, but all this moisture brings a lushness that outstrips other lush islands. Everwhere you look is a riot of leaves, flowers, birds and butterflies. Lacking white beaches Dominica is not developed towards tourism, but gains by remaining unspoiled and a nature lover's dream with two unique species of parrots.

Martinique

This is France in the tropics. The language is French, with little concession to any other except the local patois. It is heavily supported from the mainland, and you will be amazed by the difference between the French islands and the rest; the standard of living is higher, poverty lower. All the produce and products you recognize from your trips to France are here for you to enjoy. Prices are good as the imports are subsidized; many cruisers make Martinique a regular stop just to stock up on the French wines, cheeses and other goodies. The local cuisine is very French with strong Creole overtones.

It may be our imagination but the attitude towards cruisers seems a little cooler than on other islands. On the plus side, however, top marks go to the French Customs Office, the best in the Caribbean; with their ease and speedy form-filling protocols, you're through in minutes.

The island is the largest in the Windwards and rated one of the most beautiful, claiming the largest variety of flowers and shrubs. It is certainly one of the most fertile, producing a wide assortment of tropical fruits and vegetables in abundance, including the difficult to grow pineapple. St. Anne, at the southern tip, has all the flavor of a Provençal village in the tropics.

St. Lucia

A sparkling diamond-shaped island, St. Lucia was another island that went back and forth between France and England. Nevertheless, 200 years ago the British fleet had their headquarters at the northern end, under the control of Admiral George Rodney who gave his name to the bay at the north end. The British fleet is said to have hidden in the tiny bay at Marigot, behind a spit of palms, so successfully that the pursuing French sailed right on by. What most people remember about St. Lucia, however, is the truly amazing twin pinnacles of the Pitons; these two narrow cones of rock shoot out of the water to rise to over 2000 feet and seem to grow higher as you approach. As a tonic for your nerves or just for sheer indulgence try the hot springs baths in Soufrière.

St. Vincent and the Grenadines

St. Vincent sits like a mother duck with a string of ducklings straggling behind her, but there is nothing ugly about these tiny islands; they are little gems away from the glitz and glamour of the big islands.

There are about 600 islands but, counting St. Vincent, there are less than a dozen that are inhabited and the rest are barely more than scraps of rock and coral, sand and palms. St. Vincent follows the pattern of the other large islands with mountain peaks smothered in jungle and lush valleys, cliffs and crags. It was called "Isle of the Blessed" by the indigenous people with Mount Soufrière rising over 3600 feet. The volcano has erupted three times since 1902 and you can hike up to the crater to see the smouldering cone inside and the stunning view outside, if the clouds allow.

Bequia

This little island has endeared itself to cruising yachtsmen for more than half a century. Then the island was a whaling station and the intrepid Bequians hunted their prey in open boats. This is hardly surprising when you consider that their forebears were North American whalers and Scottish farmers and fishermen. Now these industrious people build beautiful wooden boats. For the cruiser, Bequia has a quaint charm all its own and, despite its miniature size, manages to provide most things for yachtsmen. Daffodil will come to your boat with water, fuel and laundry. Frangipani will handle your mail while the Gingerbread House restaurant on the waterfront will have you thinking you've wandered through the looking glass.

Mustique

When Colin Tennant (now Lord Glenconnor) bought this tiny island in the 1950s he intended it as a retreat for his family and friends. Gorgeous houses were built with beautiful grounds, tennis courts and swimming pools. He gave one particularly lovely house to the late Princess Margaret as a wedding present. Later the island was sold to a selected number of wealthy people, and is now governed by a committee of owners. It was a favorite retreat for Princess Margaret; other property is owned by Mick Jagger and David Bowie. You can anchor and walk round the island, and, if you are feeling flush, dine at the Cotton House, once a plantation house but now an elegant hotel. You can dawdle over a drink at the thatched Basil's Bar perched on stilts over the water and hope to see a celebrity.

Canuan, Mayreau and Union Island

These three islands, with Bequia, are the largest in the Grenadines, after St. Vincent under whose jurisdiction they fall. They are simple, but all offer

Despite its tiny size, cruisers of all nationalities gravitate to Bequia for Christmas and the place buzzes with activity. Midnight on New Year's Eve is celebrated in several time zones.

something, be it a pretty anchorage, good snorkeling or handy Customs check-in (Union Island).

Tobago Cays

This group of minute uninhabited islands lie in the lee of a double horse-shoe reef. Though they become more popular with each season, this is a Must Do on any cruiser's list. Follow the guidebook's chartlet to thread your way around the reefs to the west and wriggle through the pass into the anchorage to find a spot. Here you will face out over the reef, lying steady to your ground tackle with nothing between you and Africa. Come with plenty of stores for you'll want to stay for days.

Palm Island, Petit St. Vincent

These are two tiny scraps of islands, privately owned. Visitors are welcome. Palm Island was called Prune Island until it was developed by John and Mary Caldwell. John Caldwell wrote the best-selling book *Desperate Voyage*, in which he fought against incredible odds to join his wife Mary in Australia after World War II. He got rid of the mosquitoes and land crabs and planted palm trees in Palm Island.

Grenada

Although discovered by Columbus on his third voyage to the West Indies in 1498, Grenada remained unaffected for the next 150 years due to the fierce Caribs who discouraged visitors or ate them. France finally succeeded in establishing the town of St. George and held it for 100 years until the British captured it in 1762. France recaptured it but ceded it to Britain in 1783. Then followed the familiar story of importing African slave labor to work the sugar plantations. Grenada gained independence in 1974 but with political unrest and a coup d'état that resulted in the murder of the leader, U.S. troops invaded the island. Since then this mountainous and beautiful island has been largely unscarred and remains a pleasant place to visit. Spices are its chief claim to fame, for it is the world's second major producer of nutmeg and mace. Citrus fruit, cocoa, bananas and cinnamon are also grown. Visit the nutmeg factory at Dougalston on the west coast to see how the nutmeg is dried and sorted, using methods and tools that have not changed in 150 years.

Barbados

Out on its own to the east, Barbados enjoys a certain exclusivity. First discovered by Portuguese explorers in 1536, it was colonized by the British about 90 years later and it remained British until its independence in 1966. Nearly three and a half centuries of British influence have left their mark, and English traditions still hold sway including afternoon tea plus cricket in the summer, and polo in the winter. Though it is still considered appropriate to dress for dinner–some restaurants requiring jacket and tie for men–the atmosphere is decidedly non-stuffy and the Bajan hospitality is warm.

Sugar and rum–the Mount Gay (the sailor's favorite rum) distillery is located on the island–have always been two of the island's principal products while recently discovered reserves of oil and natural gas, plus tourism, have added to the economy.

Trinidad and Tobago

Trinidad

Trinidad has a long history of association with the United Kingdom and the culture still has strong British overtones. After 300 years of indifferent Spanish rule, Trinidad was captured by the British in 1797 under whose sovereignty it developed, joining with Tobago as a single country and gaining independence in 1962.

Oil was first produced in 1911. During World War II Trinidad was one of the major suppliers of oil for British ships and today its petrochemical industry accounts for about a quarter of the country's GDP. One of the by-products is the invention, in the 1940s, of "Pan" music, played on the beaten-out tops of oil drums. Calypso, songs with satirical and political lyrics, was also invented here shortly thereafter.

In the south west of the island lies the Pitch Lake, the largest natural, regenerating lake of asphalt whose product covers roads all over the world. Trinidad is a rum producer and the home of Angostura Bitters, an aromatic and alcoholic (44.7% alc./vol) flavoring used in cooking, rum punch and gin (Pink Gin).

Trinidad's capital, Port-of-Spain, is a bustling town at any time of the year, but positively erupts with festivities during the annual Carnival. Trinidad is particularly well organized for cruisers at Carnival time with seminars and transport laid on to all the many fascinating events in the run up to the final two days of parades and pantomimes. Whereas in other islands carnival is a spectator sport, in Trinidad participation is encouraged.

From Christmas onward the various competing bands display the costumes for this year's event. You choose which band to support and buy your costume. On the big day you join your band and "play pretty mas(querade)."

You need staying power, for the parade supporters of each band can run to hundreds and the masqueraders walk, stamp, dance and sway their way all through the streets to the accompaniment of very loud pan music. Reaching the open air grand stand in the Queen's Park Savannah they make a slow progress across the huge stage and off the other side. It takes the whole day and is not for the faint hearted, but I never heard anyone say they didn't enjoy it immensely, players and spectators alike.

Among the cruising fraternity there are plenty of events centered around the yards, with dinghy and cruiser racing – with and without fancy dress: Quiz nights and pot lucks, music concerts and jazz nights. Many cruisers return year after year for Carnival, combining it with the annual haul-out, though not much work gets done during the festivities, and some stalwarts organize the bussing of cruisers to all the events. Chaguaramas, at the northwest end, is a mecca for cruisers, offering a choice of yards and marine services.

A visit to the Asa Wright Nature Sanctuary in Trinidad's rain forest will reward you with many interesting sightings plus a day of deliciously cool mountain air, and equally delicious lunch in the Estate House Restaurant.

Tobago

After Trinidad's almost frenetic pace of life, Tobago is a stroll in the park. The island, largely by-passed until recently by various owners, lies slightly to the east and north of its big sister and benefits from being in clearer Atlantic waters, bringing divers from around the world. Trinidadians call it the Holiday Island and come over by ferry, even for the weekend to enjoy the quiet beaches and picture-postcard vistas. Being against wind and current the island remains unsophisticated and unspoiled with few cruising boats (see Chapter 3).

Both Trinidad and Tobago boast an abundance of rare wild life: 400 bird species and 700 different orchid species give you an idea of the island's special environment.

3

Cruising the Islands

"All plans set in Jell-O" sums up how cruisers predict their movements for the next day, week, month, etc. While most have a rough idea of where they want to be and when, the plan is always open to revision in the light of outside influences. Enforcing a rigid itinerary can lead to making a passage in less than perfect conditions. Having crew arrive in one island with a return flight from another is fine as long as there is plenty of time to allow for the unexpected. From experience, we've found it better if visitors come and go from the same place and their holiday cruising is planned around the immediate area. Enthusiastic guests may come out with the idea of a different island every day plus two dives before dinner. This seldom works for the

Speedwell of Cowes *sitting comfortably in a quiet corner of Simpson Bay Lagoon; her large awning is set and the dinghy is hoisted on davits.*

best holiday. Sailing to a tight schedule defeats the purpose of cruising. Adjust to Island Time.

Most full time cruisers are couples and their schedule usually consists of "day hopping" up and down the island chain with plenty of days, even weeks, at anchor in between. Few cruisers actually hand steer for any but the necessary maneuvers. There are occasions when it's fun to con the ship in a breeze, tweaking the rig to get the last ounce of power but, by and large, cruisers are very laid back about their sailing and don't like to push the boat or gear–unless they spot that the other fellow might be gaining. On the other hand, they might just let him go, they have nothing to prove.

Sailing

Sailing in the Caribbean is pretty straightforward once you understand the system. Offshore, the wind is invariably from east-northeast to east-southeast at about 15–25 knots, night and day; sometimes a little more, sometimes a little less.

The channel between each island is usually quite lively as the one-knot northwesterly setting current accelerates between the land masses. This can put up quite a chop. Tides, between 12 and 18 inches, may dampen the current a little on the flood but can also cause tide rips.

Coming out from behind a headland, one can get a surprise and it may be more prudent to lay off a little until past the point; this might set you down a bit on your destination but once in its lee you can motor up comfortably. Some channels have a worse reputation and it is usually the mountainous islands that cause the most acceleration of wind and current; cruising guides give details of best passage headings between islands.

Many of the islands are graced with high mountains. These give a considerable wind shadow and you may find yourself enjoying a boisterous sail to your next island and then sliding to a crawl once in its lee. Motoring plays a large part in island hopping in the Windward chain, while the mountains can throw down some interesting gusts just when you're least expecting them.

In the lee, the winds tend to ease a little at night and early risers may find an almost windless dawn. As the air temperature rises, the wind pipes up and, if there is a high barometric pressure to the north, it may bring gusty spells. There will be days when the winds are light, 10 knots or so; this is the time to make passages to windward.

There's not much work for the spinnaker in the Caribbean from Antigua south as the wind is mostly on or ahead of the beam. Even with the wind that blows predictably every day more or less from the east, squalls and gusts can come out of nowhere and a spinnaker with poles and guys could prove a liability.

Some passage notes

Montserrat is an active volcano whose status, with regard to safety, is constantly changing. It is periodically forbidden to anchor or sail close to the east of the island and sailing on the downwind side could result in ash damage. Check local news before approaching.

To make Tobago from Chaguaramas, Trinidad, the shortest course appears to be from Boca de Monos straight over to Store Bay on Tobago's southwest shore but this is into the teeth of 1–3 knots of current and the prevailing wind. Better leave in the early morning (before the wind pipes up) from Scotland Bay and motor along the north coast, pulling in to La Vache Bay, to spend the day resting. Late that evening, motor on to 61° W or the end of the island and then make a beat for Store Bay. This cuts down the open water mileage and halfway across you'll come into the lee of Drew Bank which damps the effect of the current. Tobago is worth the effort, especially during the Angostura Race Week in May with classes for cruisers and goat races for fun.

Employ this same "evening-wind-lull-close-shore" technique to work your way back east to Trinidad from Venezuela. Time the trip around a full moon for a remarkable experience as your ship glides by this stunningly beautiful coastline.

For other inter-island passages, staying well offshore to the west gets you more wind if you are trying to get the miles in. If you are planning to by-pass one or several islands from Antigua south, consider tracking to windward of the islands where you will get clean air, little traffic and a faster passage. This is particularly relevant if you are making for Chaguaramas, Trinidad from, say, Martinique, as the windward passage gives you a better angle to fetch the Boca channel than if you had come west of Grenada. It is safe 5–10 miles off, for the wind won't fail you and you can see the sprinkling of shore lights from villages on the windward coasts.

Navigation

As nearly every island is visible from its neighbor, navigation is mostly eyeball. An early start from the end of one island will usually find you comfortably anchored at the next one by afternoon, with the biggest chore being Customs clearance at both places. Be sure to plan to arrive at your chosen anchorage in good light in order to see the bottom and avoid reefs.

The windward side of most islands is inhospitable, with few anchorages. One of the exceptions is Antigua which has harbors on all sides. Martinique has a fringing reef to the east and, once safely behind it, there are some delightfully deserted anchorages. The French charts show good detail.

Buoyage

Basically, there isn't much. Navigational marks in the Caribbean are not noted for their abundance nor reliability. What you see on the chart may have been moved, changed, added to, no longer exist, or be unlit in reality. What exists is of IALA 'B' system, whereby the red port hand marker is on the right side of the channel approaching a harbor or entrance. Red Right Returning will help you remember. In popular anchorages some of the commercial concerns (marinas, restaurants) have installed channel markers using the IALA B system but they will not appear on the charts.

Charts, pilots and guides

The Imray Iolaire series of charts on the Caribbean are very popular and used by most cruisers. The more recently introduced *Caribbean Yachting Charts*, by Nautical Charts, GmbH, also appear to be good.

For Pilots and Guides, refer to Further Reading: Cruising guides.

4

The Cruising Boat

Choosing a boat for Caribbean or bluewater cruising is a mix of budget, brains and blind love. Leaving aside your starter castle, personal Learjet or your daughter's wedding, the day you purchase your boat is likely to be one of the most expensive days of your life. You'll want to get the best deal you can.

The "perfect" cruising boat, like a lot of other things in life, probably doesn't exist, but by analyzing your needs, assessing your budget and studying the market you should be able to get the best for your purpose. Below are some points to consider for your Best Boat specification; prioritize them as you please:

Buyer's checklist

- What's the top price?
- New or second hand?
- What length, design, hull material?
- What systems will you install and how will you power them?
- How many people (and their ages) will be aboard all the time or for visits?
- How long do you plan to be away? More people + more time = more stowage/weight.
- How will sleeping arrangements work out?
- Is there a berth for everyone without one crew member having to clamber over another to stand watch? What is a tolerable squeeze for the annual summer holiday could become an impossible crush for longer.
- With children aboard is there space for them to play, stow their toys and do school work? Will they be secure in their bunks on passage without attention?

Cruising with children

If you will be cruising with children, canvassing other sailing families will usually bring a flood of advice. Consult the children themselves, also. Rabidly enthusiastic parents sometimes unwittingly steamroller their less-than-eager children and the opinions and needs of the younger crew should be explored, understood and catered for, to ensure that life aboard is enjoyable for all.

Babies don't care where they are as long as Mom is around, and seldom remember much about the trip. But from around five years onward, cruising can be a very positive experience for children; education by any of the

Herman Melville looks ready to go with dinghy lashed on deck, sail cover off and a bimini shading the cockpit.

excellent correspondence courses usually puts them on a par, or ahead, of their peers by the time they reach high school, with some extra abilities as well. By the early teens many children then need the cut and thrust of shore-based education with their peers, and all the facilities, such as team sports.

Gwenda Cornell writes comprehensively about raising children afloat in her book *Cruising with Children*. Lisa Copeland chronicles her circumnavigating with husband Andy and three young sons in *Cruising for Cowards*.

Chartering a boat

If you just want to test the waters then chartering a boat for a week or two will give you a glimpse of the cruising life on a boat you manage yourself or with a skipper. Some companies offer a one-way arrangement that allows you to travel further without the worry of the return trip. Sunsail, the Moorings and Barefoot are just some of the charter companies offering mono and multihull boats in the area. See useful addresses.

Buying a boat

Price

Whatever number bracket you have in your head, be prepared to top it. With the best willpower in the world, there's always going to be something just right and just over budget with the persuasive allure of a honey jar to a bear. Having paid for your boat and got it to the Caribbean, you will probably want to add some things you hadn't thought of, or items which take on greater importance in your new environment.

Equipment and systems fail with increased use or from poor design; funds will be needed to finance repairs or replacements. Be prepared to allot a substantial portion of your cruising budget on maintenance plus faxes and telephone calls to manufacturers and suppliers; add shipping and cost (and plenty of time) into your calculations.

New or used?

There's no doubt that taking possession of a minty new boat is heady stuff but, if you have the time to look around, the second-hand market will reveal a wide choice of craft and you'll get a lot more for your money. There are some real bargains to be had.

Chartering a boat—the one-way option

Bareboat charters are extremely popular in the Caribbean. A typical charter however is one or two weeks, just enough time to sample this alluring region of palm-fringed islands, exotic cultures and steady breezes, but not nearly enough time to come to know the magic of sailing through the islands according to their own natural rythms. Worse still is that dreadful day when you've reached the halfway point of the charter. Snug in a perfect anchorage, you would like to tarry for a day or two, just to make sure you have tasted all the varieties of the local rum. Unfortunately a rigid schedule requires hauling up the anchor and reluctantly retracing your route back to the charter base.

Full-time cruising is one solution to this problem but that requires a lot of lifestyle engineering to accomplish. Another idea to consider is a long term one-way charter. Altough most charter companies charge a drop fee for one-way trips, it is usually money well spent as it allows you to cover twice as much area in the same amount of time. "One-way charters are popular at most of our Caribbean bases," explains Dorothy Geer, Public Relations Director of The Moorings. "A common route is a two- or three-week trip from St. Lucia to Grenada."

The sailing distance of this trip is around 120 miles and the wind is usually on the port beam, or depending on the season, the port quarter. Reaching before the trades is the ideal way to sail in the Caribbean, especially knowing that you don't have to turn around and sail back. In fact, most one-way routes are designed to take advantage of prevailing winds. By starting at The Moorings' base in Marigot Bay, St. Lucia, southbound sailors can gape at the island dramatic and lush landscape and enjoy a welcome lee from the usually fresh winds. Once south of St. Lucia, it is a 25-mile or four- to five-hour open water sail to the lee of St. Vincent. Below St. Vincent, the Grenadines are perched like stepping stones all the way to The Moorings' base at Mount Hardman Bay, Grenada.

There are also one-way charter opportunities in the Leeward Islands. Sunsail, with bases in Antigua and St. Martin, offers trips between the two islands. After boarding your boat in Nelson's Dockyard in English Harbour, Antigua, you can take your time sailing the 100 or so miles to St. Martin. Landfalls might include the remote island of Barbuda, with some of the Caribbean's finest beaches; St. Kitts, home to Brimstone Hill, a stone fortress known as the Gibraltar of the West Indies and sophisticated St. Barts. Steve McCrea, Sunsail's Sales Manager , sees one-way charters as more than a fad in the Caribbean. "One-ways just make sense, there is so much to see and unfortunately most people don't have enough vacation time." (See appendix 2 for Caribbean Charter Companies.)

Chartering a Boat: Your Guide to a Perfect Holiday by Chris Caswell offers a general overview of chartering and has a special section covering the Caribbean.

John Kretschmer

New

Buying new often means you can have a say in details of layout and finish
and have the chance to specify other options. This ups the satisfaction rating and makes the boat uniquely yours. New boats come with a warranty
but little else and adding the extra gear can increase your total outlay. New
boats have that Just Made look and "new" smell—and turn heads in an
anchorage.

Used

Buying a good second hand boat has a lot to recommend it; the first owner
will have hopefully ironed out most of the problems under warranty and he
or subsequent owners will have undoubtedly fitted extras. Gear will have
been tried and tested and the owner can tell you much more about how the
boat and gear handles than most yacht brokers.

Searching is fun, for the next boat you see could be *it*! With a competent
surveyor to check the ship thoroughly you may well be able to buy a larger,
better-equipped boat than you first thought. There are pitfalls, however, and
it's essential to keep a strong grip on your heart. Don't lose sight of your
goal.

Markets for pre-owned boats

While your first search for a boat is likely to be within home waters, consider looking farther afield. Popular sailing centers along the East Coast
offer a good range of cruising boats for sale. Other people's disappointments
could be your dream come true. Many an initial cruise exposes a weakness
in crew or partnerships that results in the abandonment of a project. Enter
you, with your check book and you could find a ready-to-go boat at a nice
price. While no reasonable person likes to take advantage of another's distress, you could seem heaven to someone who wants out; the market is full
of well equipped boats just waiting for a buyer. These finds tend to be located in the ports where the first long passage might have been scheduled
to start or had just ended. Contact brokers with your requirements and take
a vacation to places such as Florida, the Bahamas or the Caribbean where
some cruises fail or end. Charter companies sell off their boats and you
could pick up a good used model already in your chosen cruising ground.
The Internet is also a good place to look.

For good advice on highly recommended used cruising boats, see *Used
Boat Notebook* by John Kretschmer.

Size? Does it matter?

Not so long ago 39 feet was considered the biggest boat a couple could handle alone. Nowadays, with improved designs and gear, 60 feet and up is not considered excessive. The average today, however, is 35 to 45 feet.

A smaller boat is cheaper to buy, run and maintain. It's likely to be easier to handle and can get in where larger boats can't go. Disadvantages include cramped conditions, fewer facilities and stowage, slower passages and more susceptibility to wind and weather. A smaller boat can feel very confining in the heat.

Larger boats come with more equipment as standard, generally have an easier motion in the water, are faster, less susceptible to wind and weather. Faster passages get you where you want to be quicker and could get you out of danger–running away from bad weather instead of plowing through it. Larger boats can cost more to buy, run and maintain, though in the second-hand market you can often get a bigger boat for the price of a smaller new one.

This day-anchorage at Sandy Spit gives you the chance to play Crusoe; but it'll take you nearly five minutes to walk around your island.

What hull? Mono or multi?

There is no perfect boat for cruising as each cruiser's ideals differ. Speed may have been your priority in home waters, but fast boats can be wet and wearying, with few comforts below and your crew might not share your enthusiasm for months of primitive living. Mono and multihulls each have their devotees and choice is personal.

Multihulls are usually faster than monohulls because they are lighter. They are spacious with large cockpits and vast saloons with sit-down-and-see-out windows. Multis are usually more expensive per dollar/foot. Their renowned stability is appealing but they can and do stay inverted when flipped.

The majority of cruising boats are monohulls and there is a marked difference in the feel between different hull designs. Two boats, in the same condition, of the same length, but of different hull shapes can feel and behave differently. Described in degrees of sea kindliness, the motion of the boat under way could be the making, or not, of a successful cruise. The crew most susceptible to mal de mer should definitely take part in any trial sails.

Working up and down the islands involves windward sailing. A full keel boat has directional stability but may be difficult going astern and, with that extra wetted area, is slower. A modern hull with spade rudder and deep fin keel will generally go faster, turn quicker and feel more responsive at the helm. It may also have a more lively motion.

Unlike the Bahamas, where our 6-foot draft made for some nerve tingling navigation at times, your boat's draft is unlikely to cause problems in the Caribbean. There's seldom a pass or anchorage that is prohibited because of insufficient depth.

Stowage

This is the perennial problem with cruisers—there's always more stuff than space to stow it. Apart from food and tools, which are dealt with separately, it's all the "house and home" items that need careful planning. Children aren't the only ones with toys. There are few cruisers who are content just to sail and maintain the boat, and have no other interests.

There is an amazing pool of talent among long-term cruisers that seems to cover every skill imaginable from the simplest pencil sketching to full scale oil painting, needlework, crafts, music making, wood carving and more. Mechanics, shipwrights, carpenters, electricians and computer buffs abound. The professions are well represented with doctors, dentists, lawyers and others. Very few of these people manage to leave home without bringing some of the tools of their trade with them and, along the way, much more gets added. It is important to make provision for all your toys and accoutrements plus plenty of space for books.

Computers play an increasing part in cruising life today. Electronics don't like the marine atmosphere of damp and salt and tend to die suddenly. Secure, dry stowage with silica gel packs in a sealed container will help to preserve the hardware. Sealable plastic bags are better than nothing. The hermetically sealed plastic boxes are ideal for the storage of cameras, computers, slides and other moisture-sensitive equipment. They also make sturdy lockable cases.

Additional stowage for soft goods such as clothes and toys can be gained with bags made of sturdy fabric and screwed under the deckhead over bunks at the foot end.

Lightweight plastic containers, such as used for distilled water, will, with the boat's motion, chafe a minute hole leaking the contents into the bilge. With chemicals, the result could be dangerous and you may not notice the loss until a nasty smell arises. Decant fluids into high-density plastic containers.

Galley stowage is always at a premium. The traditional system of a net hammock suspended at both ends tends to swing and bruise the contents. Netting suspended under the galley deck head, in four corners and edged with a bungy cord, provides a stable airy housing for more than just food.

Six people on a charter boat with their flight allowance will probably bring more than 2½ hundredweight (132 kilos) aboard. That's before stowing the food, soft drinks, beer and booze for a week. A cruiser will also bring toys, books, hobby

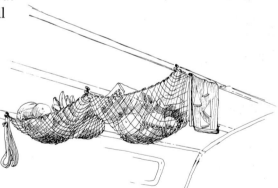

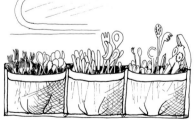

Extra stowage can be added almost anywhere with the use of fabric pockets and net hammocks. Thread the net with bungy cord and secure it at four corners for stability.

items, tools and spares plus linen, clothes and galley items. Few cruisers could pack all their belongings into their flight luggage. Most boats, when changing to cruising mode, will add 2–4 tons of additional gear and will raise the waterline by 6 inches; a lightweight production boat may not be designed for such loading.

You're not free of paperwork, either. Apart from ship's papers and passports for each crew member, there are Customs forms, tax returns, bank and credit card statements, letters to/from official bodies, equipment suppliers, insurance companies, and personal correspondence. If you have property or business back home, it will need some sort of maintenance. All this generates paper that needs keeping in a safe, dry place.

Some points to note for a cruising interior

- Is there adequate and easily accessible stowage for food stores that does not require lifting heavy sole boards while on passage?
- Is the chart table big enough to take a chart without folding or creasing the corners?
- Are there adequate handholds for safety on passage?
- Can you clip on your safety harness before leaving the companionway?
- Are there at least 13 feet of book shelf?
- Is there stowage for storing charts flat? Rolled charts are difficult to work on. Paper is heavy and charts can run to hundreds with

extended cruising, so the drawer or locker needs to be secure.
- Are the sleeping arrangements adequate? Regrouping the saloon cushions over the lowered saloon table for a bed each night, only to put it all back next morning, quickly becomes tiresome.
- Are the clothes' lockers well ventilated?
- Will the galley be reasonably comfortable in a seaway?
- Can you see yourself producing meals in it day after day?
- Is there room for all members of the crew to have their own personal space?

Ventilation

A factor often overlooked by those who have not cruised in tropical waters is the need for adequate ventilation below. The need to force air through the boat to keep temperatures bearable below cannot be stressed too highly. Dorades with swivelling cowls serve this purpose well as they can be left open while sailing and in rain. Without good ventilation it can become very oppressive below when hatches must be closed.

Unfortunately, the very openings that allow the passage of air also admit less desirable elements such as insects. Mosquitoes and no-see-ums can be a real torment in the tropics and it only takes one biter to ruin your night.

Screening the hatches and the main hatch in particular, is tricky unless your hatches have custom screens fitted. There are various solutions. While at anchor, nylon dress-weight netting hemmed with tiny lead beads can be draped over open hatches. The weights should keep it from being blown away and the hatch can be dropped when it rains. The disadvantage is that one has to go on deck to deploy the net initially though it can be retrieved through the hatch.

Some dorades come with a fine wire mesh which works well but soon becomes clogged with dust and must be cleaned often or the flow of air is restricted.

Funnelling wind below is essential for interior comfort. Note the canvas hatch covers and one of the six dorades on Honey Jar.

A Windscoop hood incorporating fly screening can be tailored to fit with studs to hold it securely but again must be deployed from on deck and removed before the hatch can be shut. The main hatch is more of a problem as a fly screen needs to be of a design to permit the easy passage of people but not insects. A battened screen tethered at the top that can be pushed up and out of the way, like a Roman blind, works well as long as there are reinforcing patches to protect the netting from hand damage.

Fans are essential in the tropics. There may not be a breeze at anchor and the unannounced rain showers and squalls will have you opening and closing the hatches constantly. At sea it is not always safe to have hatches open and fans provide a welcome current of air. Hella fans have a low power consumption and are quiet enough to be left on while you sleep. These two desirable qualities do not come cheap but the fans earn their price, running for years, if kept free of dust.

The main hatch is not easy to bug-proof. Here a net and fabric blind concertinas up with a cord pulled from either inside or out.

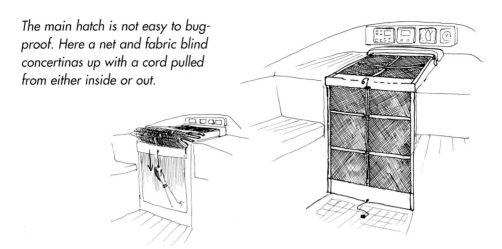

The galley

After the navigation station, the galley is arguably the most important space in the boat. Cooks have absolute right in the galley and everything should be ordered to their demands. The stove will be gimballed but the reinforced connecting pipe for the propane should be inspected regularly for wear, for it moves each time the stove swings. With an 8-second roll on a 20-day passage, the boat will roll 216,000 times. The gimbal fitting should be secured.

A metal tray, preferably stainless steel, about half the width of the stove and sitting on the fiddle rails, makes a good platform for preparing hot drinks. Mugs of hot liquids can be safely left on it for they don't move or slop. Paper towels in the bottom make a good drip catcher. Even in quite rough conditions it is possible to prepare drinks in safety. Measure the inside of the fiddle rail from back to front and buy a stainless steel meat pan or tray to fit with a lip to suspend it on the rail over the burner.

Above: A bum-strap in the galley leaves the cook with both hands free.
Left: a stainless steel tray fits snugly between the fiddles and holds drinks better than in the sink.

Barbara works in her compact, well-planned galley aboard Kelly's Eye. *A fold-out shelf gives extra space.*

This tray has been one of the most useful items in my boat galleys for over 20 years. Being metal, the tray is quite safe over a burner that is turned off but still hot and will keep china and ceramic plates warm; it is easily removed if both burners are needed.

On deck

Dark hulls get much hotter than white. Always lying head-to-east, the starboard side is hotter in any color; site the refrigerator to port if possible.

Teak decks are pretty when new, but get too hot to stand on under a tropical sun. Teak is never salt free to sit on or to collect rainwater. Teak sloughs off gray "felt" which gathers in corners and ports. Tropical sun causes it to expand and contract more quickly; seams open and maintenance is ongoing. It is recommended to wash teak decks with sea water twice a day to keep them from drying out.

The rig
Consider the following points:

- Can I reef easily and safely in windy conditions?
- What modifications would assist short handed sailing?

With any second-hand boat, have the rig examined by a qualified surveyor or rigger who knows your intended cruising plans. Have necessary repairs or replacements done well before leaving home.

The cockpit
The cockpit is a popular area in the Caribbean cruising boat and, apart from being the driving seat, it is the living room, sun lounge, terrace, and party room all in one. Big cockpits are great for those balmy anchorages but imagine it inclined at 20°, pitching in high seas when the autopilot has died and you're faced with hours or days of hand steering through deteriorating conditions. Check for enough bracing points for foot- and hand-holds plus padeyes for safety harness attachment. Coamings should be deep enough to support your back while on watch as well as sitting comfortably in port.

The foredeck awning catches the breeze while the main awning, with side curtains, shades the deck. Dorade ventilators, six on this 40-footer, keep fresh air moving through the boat.

Instant awning

An "instant" awning that can be deployed quickly and easily anywhere about the boat is useful. Take a 13-foot length of 54-inch dress-weight cotton fabric, printed on one side only, preferably in blue. Turn a simple hem on all four sides. Using light line ⅛-inch tie 1 yard lengths at each corner (a) using a reef knot, the corners need no reinforcing, for the gathering of the fabric at the knot is sufficient. Use a simple clove hitch to secure to lifelines, boom end, rigging, etc., with the free end in a bight; one pull will release the line. If you are really keen, sew a length of light braid or ribbon across the middle of the cloth, along the width, forming a loop at each side (b) with lines for additional securing. This cheap simple awning can then be strung, pale side out, wherever it is needed to give instant shade such as when doing a job on deck. On the hard, tie it from the toe rail to the ground and shade the hull on the sunny side to help keep the boat cool while out of the water. Being of lightweight cloth, it is quick and easy to deploy or take down, roll small and stow.

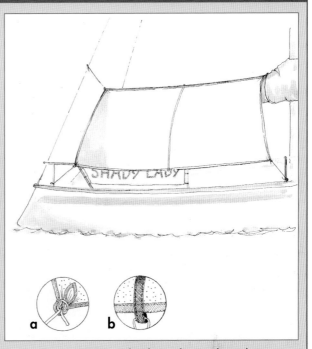

Cockpit cushions are best covered with a waterproof fabric that wipes clean, some cushions come ready sealed with a plastic "skin." Tailor-made canvas covers look pretty but keeping the fabric clean and salt free is difficult.

A dodger is essential to protect the open main hatch from rain and spray and should be deep enough to keep the crew on watch out of the weather when underway. Caribbean night watches can be chilly after the heat of the day and the down draft from the main shuttles the rain into the cockpit.

Shade

Shade in the cockpit is essential for comfort. Shoveling snow in the depths of a New England winter, you might think that shade is the last thing you want but the tropical sun will start to prickle uncomfortably in minutes as the burning rays destroy your skin. A bimini, sturdy enough to remain in place while sailing, is a popular fitting on many cruising boats and can also make a useful rain catcher.

An awning that covers more than just the cockpit will make life below more comfortable when at anchor for longer than an afternoon. Most awnings are made to order for each boat as owner's requirements are different. Awnings are also useful for catching rainwater. With water being readily available in the Caribbean, at a price, catching water might seem in the same bracket as oil lamps and leadlines but the rain is free.

Outboard motors, containers carried on deck and even the dinghy all last longer if protected from the relentless UV damage with a cover. Antigua, Sint Maarten and Trinidad are top favorites for canvas work.

5

Equipment

Priorities

The amount and type of equipment carried on a cruising boat depends very much on the type of cruiser. There are the die-hard traditionalists whose Spartan boat would be recognized by Joshua Slocum: kerosene for light and cooking, a basin for dishes, and a bucket for the rest. Even the navigation lights might be oil. That's fine if it's your choice but more and more cruising boats these days are becoming a home away from home. That's fine too but the conveniences don't run on candles and power has to be made to service them.

Auxiliary engines

It is assumed that most boats will have an inboard auxiliary engine. Diesel fuel quality is generally good in the Caribbean and filters and oil are available as well as mechanics for service and repair in the larger islands. Fan belts and impellers can also be found although you should carry several spares for your particular model since both items are more likely to fail on passage than in a handy anchorage.

Oil in the Caribbean is usually multi-grade 15/40 or 40W. Engines run hotter in the tropics. Most cruisers use 40W with success. Disposing of waste oil can pose a problem but most large marinas will take yours if you are using their services. Not all fuel docks take waste oil and you might need to search for a suitable disposal site.

The heat from an engine or generator does not dissipate from the boat as easily in the Caribbean as it does in cooler waters and engine block temperature continues to rise and radiate like storage heaters for some time after use. Adequate engine room ventilation will help to prevent the heat from radiating into the boat.

Refrigeration

No longer just for the largest yachts, refrigeration has the reputation of causing the most aggravation; it also uses a lot of power but there are few cruisers without it. Units can be driven from compressors: engine-mounted, generator-driven or 12-volt and they can be water or air cooled. Skippers running their engine daily, such as in the case of charter boats, might prefer engine-driven compressors and those with wind and solar powered boats might favor 12-volt systems.

Insulation is the most important factor in efficient refrigeration. A minimum of 4 inches (10 centimeters) all round is needed and 6 inches (15 centimeters) is ideal if space allows, but insulation is only as good as its weakest part.

Most boat refrigerators have top opening, which means delving to the depths to find what you want. A unit with front as well as top opening is ideal for access but sheds the cold more quickly.

Insulated cool boxes, either built-in or free standing, can be used but will require an almost daily supply of ice to keep food safe in the tropical heat. At US $3-5 a bag for ice this would not seem the cheap option for a boat on a small budget, apart from the restrictions of having to stay near a source. With no built-in refrigerator it might be easier to go without food cooling and stick to vegetables and canned food.

Though power-hungry, a freezer extends the time between shopping trips—a common cruising aim—and widens the choice and life of foods which can be stored on board. (See *Marine Electrical and Electronics Bible* by John C. Payne for all the information you need to select, install, maintain and troubleshoot any electrical or electronic system you have on board.)

Air conditioning

A power-hungry item to have permanently installed, air conditioning is generally only found on bigger boats and powered by generator or shore power. You might, however, consider it as a temporary measure if you haul out for any time. In Trinidad, for instance, cruisers spend a lot of time on the hard while refitting but the climate is enervatingly humid in a dusty yard. Renting a unit that fits over a hatch to keep the interior of the boat cool makes a world of difference in getting a lot of work done below, plus sleeping comfortably at night.

Bottled gas

Propane is the most popular method of cooking on board today. Sometimes called cooking gas, it is readily available throughout the islands where your

Limited tankage is overcome with extra water and fuel in containers, securely lashed on deck. It is not an ideal arrangement, but better than running short.

bottle will be refilled but not exchanged. The gas used to refill bottles is a mixture of propane and butane and should be used on a system with a propane regulator. Butane regulators are not suitable, and butane bottles cannot be refilled except in Trinidad.

Most U.S. cruising boats use aluminum bottles as the steel version is of thin gauge and generally used for domestic barbecues, rusting quickly under marine conditions.

Tankage

While diesel and water are readily available in the Caribbean, large capacity tankage for both will mean fewer stops. With a minimum drinking requirement of 3½ pints (2 liters) per person per day in the tropics, plus allowing water for cooking, dishwashing and personal use, you'll need a minimum of one gallon per person per day of the voyage. For safety, allowing 3 weeks for the trip, for two people you will need to carry about 50 gallons (110 liters) while maintaining strict water rations. It's quite common to see smaller boats with decks strung with plastic water containers.

It is unwise to cut down on drinking water when in the tropics and washing only with salt water can cause skin irritation (see Chapter 17).

Holding Tanks

A holding tank is essential if you are cruising in US waters (US Virgins, etc.). The alternative is to go three miles offshore to use your marine toilet—obviously not practical and no authority is going to believe your claim that you pop out to sea from the anchorage each time nature calls. While the Caribbean is getting more pollution conscious, it is still permissible to discharge overboard though one yacht was turned out of Tobago recently through lack of a holding tank. As Tobago doesn't have a pump-out station this seemed a little harsh. But it doesn't pay to argue with local officials.

Holding tanks are mandatory in the US. Fit a "Y" valve so that you have the option to discharge overboard once outside the three-mile limit. Fit a deck plate for pumping out at marinas in the US. It is usually straight forward and the charge is minimal; sometimes it is even free.

Spares and tools

Most boatyards in the Caribbean can supply engineers and technicians and they should have the necessary tools to carry out maintenance work. Most cruisers carry a comprehensive range of tools to fit their particular equipment plus stainless fixings, screws, nuts and bolts, washers, etc, in a range of sizes. Engineers may not have the necessary parts to repair your equipment so essential parts should be held on board, otherwise parts may need to be imported.

Make sure you carry the relevant operation and service manuals plus parts lists applicable to all the major items on your boat. Your chosen boatyard may not have the necessary technical information on the idiosyncrasies of your particular model. We have found it useful to keep a detailed list of all equipment on board with model, part and serial numbers, address, e-mail, fax and telephone number of manufacturers or suppliers plus the name of a contact if possible.

These days U.S. and metric sizing dominates. Secure storage of spares and tools is vital.

Windvane steering

Cruisers don't do much hand steering and the majority of self-steering time on cruising boats is done by an autopilot and a lesser amount with a windvane. Both, if chosen to match the weight and balance of the boat, will manage very well steering on the given setting. In heavy weather the windvane will manage better and consume none of the ship's power, whereas the autopilot will labor and consume a lot of amperes. In light winds, particularly downwind, the autopilot will cope better than the wandering windvane. Neither can anticipate a situation and, over the short

The presence of a windvane and wind generator usually indicate a bluewater cruiser. The pole supports radar well above the helmsman's head while two dorades ventilate the aft cabin.

course, cannot match the skill of a good helmsman. Humans need rest and relief, however, and few boats choose to go without an autopilot and many boats under 45 feet (14 metres), making long passages, sport windvane steering as well.

Windlasses and ground tackle

Anchor chain seems to get heavier as one gets older and a decent windlass will more than earn its keep. If you can run to an electric windlass, do so; you'll seldom regret not having to haul every foot by hand. It also means that the crew can, if necessary, weigh anchor without strain. Despite the advances in marine electrics, salt will inevitably affect ingress and attention to maintenance will be time well spent.

Chain is the recommended choice for an anchor rode in the Caribbean as rope may fray and will also require too much scope in popular restricted anchorages. Chain is more resistant to wear even though, with continued use, it will lose its galvanizing and need to be regalvanized or replaced (see Chapter 12).

Anchor wash

Caribbean sand usually washes off as the chain comes up from the sea bed but there are anchorages where it will come up fouled with the sort of stuff you will not want on the chain, on your foredeck or your hands. Failing a deck wash, a small bucket with a stout lanyard can be dipped over the side for rinsing water. The old fashioned style of lavatory brush with a loop of twisted metal trapping a fringe of plastic bristles works better than a scrubber for dislodging mud off the links. Stout leather gloves are good for handling chain fouled with mud or barnacles.

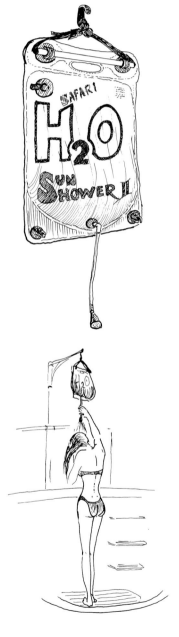

Shore lines

You can never have too many lines on a boat. Having a long line for running ashore from the stern is useful in some anchorages to keep the boat's head to the swell or if the anchorage is confined but popular; 200 feet (60 metres) is a useful length.

Deck showers and spray bottles

If your water tanks will allow, a fresh water shower on the aft deck is a great boon. Not just for après-swim and showers but rinsing dive gear, oilies etc. A solar shower, hung from the backstay or similar high point, is a cheaper option and works well in the tropical sun.

A gallon (or larger) garden pressure spray bottle lashed to the stern pulpit makes a handy fresh water rinse after swimming. Even if you have a fresh water shower fitted, the spray bottle is useful also as a hand and foot rinse when coming back aboard after a trip ashore in the dinghy to lessen the amount of salt and dirt tracked below. Keeping everything below decks as salt free as possible helps to prolong the active life of sensitive electronics and keeps the interior sweet smelling. Rinsing snorkels and

A solar shower is a refreshing finish after swimming and handy for washing and cooling down.

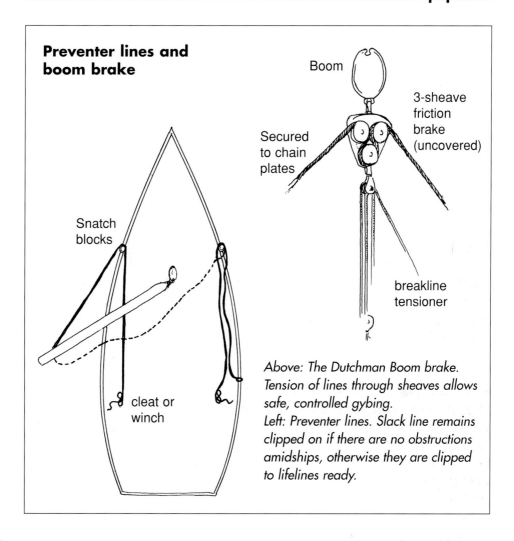

Preventer lines and boom brake

Boom

3-sheave friction brake (uncovered)

Secured to chain plates

Snatch blocks

breakline tensioner

cleat or winch

Above: The Dutchman Boom brake. Tension of lines through sheaves allows safe, controlled gybing.
Left: Preventer lines. Slack line remains clipped on if there are no obstructions amidships, otherwise they are clipped to lifelines ready.

other swimming gear after use extends their life and stops them from getting sticky.

The garden spray bottle also has the advantage of being portable so that ports, hatches and cockpit can be rinsed free of salt after a boisterous passage. It is useful below for a spring cleaning of lockers and bilge areas below the sole.

Boarding ladders and passerelles

A ladder that hangs from the toerail is handy for boarding from the dinghy. A swim ladder needs at least two rungs below the water to make it easy to climb aboard.

This heavyweight sewing machine earns its keep as I make another new awning.

Some docks and marinas offer only stern-to mooring, while others offer pontoons for boarding the vessel. If you intend to lie stern-to, a passerelle or other boarding plank will be useful. A large fender board can also be used for this purpose where appropriate.

Mast steps

These are very useful in the Caribbean as crew can nip aloft to con the ship through narrow passages and they are a good safety device for emergency work aloft as well as for taking photos. It is not recommended to use the windlass or a powered winch to raise a person, in case there is gear failure or lines or fingers get trapped.

Mast steps also encourage regular maintenance inspections.

Courtesy flags and ensigns

You will need the yellow 'Q' flag plus the courtesy flags for all the islands you intend to visit; this means virtually all the islands if you are planning a season in the Caribbean. They can be purchased on larger islands but it might be cheaper to bring them from home. It is not correct to enter the waters of a new island without flying the courtesy flag at the starboard spreader and, if spotted, you could find yourself unpopular with the authorities.

Sails

If the mainsail is more than five years old, is lightweight and is showing signs of wear, consider making it a "get you home" spare and go for a newer, better cut cruising weight sail that will be your workhorse for the years to come. A reputable sailmaker will advise on the best weight for your boat size and tropical cruising. You may be surprised at how heavy a cruising sail is if you've only been used to inshore weight sails; new halyards may also be indicated. Sails usually fail under adverse conditions and that's not the time you'll want to get out the sewing kit to struggle with wet and salty fabric with a negative attitude—its and yours.

Most cruising boats have roller-furling headsails and yours should be overhauled before a cruise. Roller gear has come a long way and most of the popular makes are highly reliable. Check the sacrificial cloth along the leech and foot and beef up for tropical sun. White reflects the heat but at night the reflection of a powerful flashlight off the white cloth can be blinding. Darker colors get hotter and seem to deteriorate sooner.

Downwind sails won't be much use as from Antigua southward, winds are mostly on or forward of the beam. Northward and in the Virgins, lightweight sails can fly again. A snuffer or sock to de-power these sails is useful, for squalls can come up suddenly.

Sail care and repair

Tropical sun and salt are particularly hard on sails and they need extra protection. Unless you have in-mast furling, put on the cover the moment the sail is lowered. In the Caribbean, each minute the sail is naked, particularly when flaked, face up on the boom, equals a week's wear; even overcast days are high in UV.

6

Dinghies & Outboards

Dinghies

The ship's tender is arguably the most important piece of moveable gear. The dinghy is the family runabout whose reliability is paramount. There will be times when you need to travel several miles to reach good diving, shopping or friends, leaving the mother ship in a safe anchorage. A stable dinghy is essential. Choosing the right one depends on budget, boat and cruising style. For passage-making it must be stowed onboard; inter-island seas can be rough, currents strong and winds gusty.

Dinghies can be hard, inflatable, folding or a combination of any or all of those. Hard dinghies, probably the cheapest option, withstand the wear and tear of crowded pontoons and being dragged up the beach. They are easily repaired, they are usually lighter than inflatables and row well; they are also less attractive to thieves. The downside is that hard dinghies tend to be less stable: getting in and out with loads of shopping becomes a practised art. They are difficult to board from the water after swimming.

A sailing rig for the dinghy might sound like a good idea but the tropical climate makes the slow passage to the dock too hot and beating back or short tacking through a busy anchorage to your boat on the far side, with cold stores, is too lengthy. For fun sailing, some cruisers carry wind-surfers but it's mainly the holiday makers who use them. Apart from children in Optimists (or similar) at yacht clubs and Hobies rented from resorts, you will seldom see any sailing dinghies belonging to cruisers.

Getting ashore can often mean getting out of and back into the dinghy over the bow, for the dinghy dock may be crowded with dinghies crammed side by side. If there's no room you may have to climb over several dinghies to reach the dock, carrying a long painter with you.

Inflatable dinghies come in many designs. Floors can be wood, fiberglass or aluminum, some folding in sections making them easier to stow. Others have an inflated floor with a keel which makes them easier to row. Lightweight inflatables have a tendency to flip, when empty, in gusty winds.

There are several makes of folding wood or fiberglass dinghies of ingenious designs that address the space and stowage problem; visit a boat show to make comparisons.

RIBs

Rigid inflatable boats are now one of the most popular types of dinghy for cruisers in the Caribbean and used almost exclusively by the charter companies. The two large pontoons attached to a V-shape rigid hull make a perfect marriage. Some have extras such as dodgers, seats, lockers for gear and lifting rings, etc. Strong towing eyes at the bow allow these tough craft to be towed in quite rough conditions, though an additional safety line is advisable.

With a suitably-sized outboard, a RIB will plane, covering long distances quickly with little wake. As load carriers they are excellent, being capacious and very stable. The large pontoons mean a relatively dry ride and make loading and boarding over the bow and from the dock easier than any other design. The down side is the price, RIBs don't come cheap even in Venezuela, but no one who squeezes the budget to buy one ever regrets it.

RIBs are heavy; work out how you will ship, stow and launch your dinghy before deciding on type. Our RIB, with a 15hp outboard, purchased in our second cruising year, was one of our best investments. Dinghies and outboards are currency, make sure yours stays with you (see Chapter 16).

With a fast stable dinghy you can get to places where the mother ship cannot go. Many of the best snorkeling and diving sites are far from a secure anchorage and it's handy to be able to whiz off a couple of miles in the dinghy with all the gear for a spot of goggling. Being able to sneak over shallow reefs, up rivers and hidden creeks gets you to places others can't reach.

Should the auxiliary engine fail, it's comforting to know that your tender can give some steerage to the mother ship when lashed alongside with a powerful outboard.

Safety

In the US Virgin Islands the Coast Guard requires that dinghies carry a (PFD) personal flotation device for each passenger.

Have a bridle made up by a rigger for lifting the dinghy, gauged so that it can be raised to the toerail or fully aboard, using the spinnaker halyard or other suitable line. Davits are a very convenient way to lift and secure the dinghy.

Five knots is the usual speed limit through busy anchorages with minimum wake. Tropical nights are pitch dark. When under way at night, show at least a white light–preferably small navigation lights that run directly off the outboard. You may have your night vision but others might not.

Dinghies are essential for island cruising. A stern line holds this dinghy and outboard off the beach, otherwise the surge would keep nudging it up on the rocks.

A light line is useful in the dinghy as a stern rope and, with a small folding grapnel anchor plus three foot of chain, will hold the dinghy off the dock or shore as well as on the reef while you snorkel or swim.

Outboards

A few cruisers row their dinghies but it's difficult work against the prevailing elements. Most chose to power their dinghy with an outboard but keep paddles or oars in case of motor failure. It seems that the more expensive outboards do reward their owners with fewer breakdowns but the choice is still personal.

With a RIB there need be little concern about the motor's weight as RIBs are very stable so the advice is to get the biggest outboard your budget will allow within the manufacturer's safety range. Caribbean waters can be choppy and with wind and current constant in one direction, loss of power could see you going west before you intended. An under powered dinghy can be agonizingly slow and is tiresome if you are trying to get a bulk purchase of stores or clean dry laundry back to the mother ship before the next deluge.

On a rigid dinghy, a tiller extension allows the solo helmsman to shift his weight forward to help keep the nose down. A hoisting arm on the stern of the mother ship will aid lifting and lowering the outboard motor, as well as any other heavy cargo. This is an essential piece of equipment for any outboard from 5hp up to avoid back strain.

Getting an outboard motor repaired in the Caribbean is seldom a problem. It is best to have your outboard serviced by the agent as he is likely to have the parts required.

7

Electrical power

Electrical power for your systems has got to come from somewhere, it has to be managed and stored. The more toys on board, the more power is needed to run them.

Diesel generators

Most boats rely on their main engine to charge the batteries that store the power. Adding a generator will leave the main engine for motive power only, and while charging batteries, the generator can make and heat water, cool the refrigerator plus power hot plates, kettle, microwave oven, vacuum cleaner, etc.

Generators usually use less fuel than the main engine, are quieter to run (except the portable on-deck kind) and don't upset the neighbors but they are costly, take space, drink fuel, and also need servicing and spares.

Most marine diesel engines have an alternator with an output sufficient to charge an engine start battery and provide some extra output for periodic basic lighting and other light loads. For most cruising boats, the electrical demands will be higher and the supplied alternator and battery capacity will probably be inadequate. A dedicated engine starting battery plus a separate battery bank for domestic services are a necessity.

Batteries

The type of batteries you install is also a matter of choice. Wet cell and gel batteries both have their devotees but the sorry truth is that most marine batteries seldom last as long as the makers claim. This can be through mismanagement or lack of understanding. Cruising batteries are worked hard, constantly charging and being discharged. The plates can sulfate quickly and the battery loses efficiency.

Wet cell batteries are cheaper to buy, their charging level is not so critical and they are more forgiving of misuse (overcharging) but they spill acid if tipped and require more attention. Gel cell batteries are more expensive to buy, have more specific charging requirements, cannot be refilled if overcharged but don't spill, require less attention and will deep cycle for longer.

AGM batteries, a newer technology, are filled with absorbent glass mat between the plates to hold the electrolyte. They are also sealed and don't spill, but are more expensive to buy and cannot be refilled if overcharged.

Intelligent charge regulators help extend battery life. Also monthly higher voltage equalization charges can help prevent plate sulfation.

Battery systems

Diesel engines, by their design, require no electrics to keep running, but a boat diesel is impossible to hand crank and power is needed to start it and to power glow plugs and sensors. Caribbean daylight is only 12 hours on average so artificial light is needed after about 6 p.m. The climate means that refrigeration and fans will be working harder, demanding more power.

It is unwise for even the smallest cruising boat to rely on only one battery to serve the engine and household needs. At least one extra battery is necessary for domestic and navigational electrics but it must be kept separate from the engine battery to avoid inadvertent discharge of both. One alternator can be made to feed two batteries, but if space permits, a better arrangement is to have two alternators; one should be larger so that it can service more than one household battery and more closely match the daily electrical requirements.

Calculate your daily expected power usage; your services battery bank should have at least three to four times this capacity.

Wind generators

In the Caribbean, harnessing the almost constant 15–25 knots of wind makes sense and wind generators in many styles are a common sight on cruising boats. You need to be aware, however, that some spots on an island's leeward side may be in a wind shadow.

A small, efficient wind generator can feed the modest power requirements of a small boat and might be all that's needed to store enough power in a battery to power the nav lights, a cabin light and a radio (for listening only).

Small-output wind generators will be totally inadequate for the boat with a greater power requirement. A manufacturer's stated output of at least 6 amps at 15-knot wind speed is the minimum to have any charging effect for most cruising boats. It is not unusual to see boats with a combination of wind generators and solar panels (see Solar Panels below).

Some of the larger units cannot be run while sailing in anything other than light winds. The portable type is tiresome, having to be alternately deployed and stowed. Ask the opinion of cruisers in a busy anchorage; experienced users are more forthright than manufacturers when it comes to the performance and shortcomings of marine gear.

Water-powered generators

The ampere wind generator is designed to take an impeller towed behind the boat. This is a very efficient means of producing power on a long passage. The impeller is quite hefty and some slight loss of boat speed may result. On short passages, a water impeller has little benefit.

Solar panels

Technology has advanced in this field but not quite as fast as one would hope and the appealing ideal of free power with no moving parts has yet to be perfected. Nevertheless, efficient and strategically placed solar panels can harness a useful amount of power.

Solar panels do not like shadow and even the thin line of standing rigging can reduce the efficiency. Bear in mind, when siting a solar panel that boats in the Caribbean always lie with the sun to starboard. Flexible panels are not as efficient and are bothersome to stow. With modest power requirements, a combination of wind and solar power may see you having the last laugh on your more profligate neighbors.

The advantage of using solar panels and wind generators is that they will be supplying power against demand, so reducing battery cycling and charging requirements. Reduced cycling gives a longer life for the batteries, in terms of years, and reduced charging saves engine/generator wear, fuel and noise. Against these benefits you must consider initial cost.

Shore power

There will be occasions when you can plug into shore power and, unless your boat is of minimalist design, it is a good idea to make provision to take advantage of this service when available. Shore power will give your

This seasoned cruising boat has solar panels on her coachroof, side deck and stern rail. There is also a wind-generator, wind vane steering and bimini.

batteries the benefit of a full charge, through a battery charger. If you are going to be along side or hauled out for any length of time, it is very convenient to be able to run lights, tools and other equipment at the flick of a switch.

Wiring a boat's electrical system is a job for a professional, but the owner must have a good appreciation of the requirements for safe installation. Before connecting, always test the source outlet for correct polarity and voltage as island systems can be unreliable and variable. Test plugs are available, but a voltmeter is a handy tool to keep aboard for testing ship's systems and other gear.

On a marina dock, the power outlet is likely to be close to your slip so a shorter cable will suffice. Hauled out in a boatyard, however, you may well need 100 feet (30 metres) or more to reach the nearest outlet.

Connecting cables are available in the Caribbean in standard lengths, commonly 25 and 50 feet (8 and 15 metres) with waterproof connections for the commonly-used U.S. system with 30 amp 125 volt 2 pole 3 wire and for larger vessels 50 amp 125/250 volt. St. Lucia has the European 32 amp 220/240 volt 3 pin. St. Martin is on 220 volts. It is worth making up adapter tails to cope with the different types of plugs fitted to different appliances. Outlets in boatyards may be 15 amp 125 volt. Always check that the supply voltage agrees with the appliance requirements; mismatch could cause meltdown. Steel and aluminum boats should be fitted with an isolating transformer. If an isolating transformer is used, adjustable tappings on input and output can be an advantage.

Caribbean power failures, known as "outages," are common but things are improving all the time as new systems are fitted. Be prepared to have work interrupted and no obvious action taken for hours. They'll fix it eventually.

Inverters and inverter/chargers

Inverters are a very useful way of converting 12- or 24-volt battery power into AC to operate equipment such as computers, printers, food mixers and other light load equipment. A small, portable inverter with an output from 150 to 1000 watts could operate a variety of equipment. For example, a 250-watt inverter could provide power for a computer and printer. Larger inverters, with outputs from 1000 to 2500 watts are built for permanent installation, with some operating as inverter chargers when connected to shore power or when running a generator.

Some of the smaller inverters, especially when used to power a computer, can cause interference on a radio. Listen to weak signals on your SSB radio on the bands and frequencies you use most, with and without the inverter on, to determine if you have an interference problem.

For a more in-depth understanding of power generating and battery management, the *Boatowners's Mechanical & Electrical Manual* by Nigel Calder and *Understanding Boat Batteries and Battery Charging* by John C. Payne will be worthwhile purchases (see Further Reading).

8

Electronics

Few cruisers would choose to go to sea today without one or several of the electronic boating goodies on offer. Apart from the obvious first choices of depth, wind and speed instruments, the next most popular is probably GPS, closely followed by an autopilot.

GPS

Although not essential for Caribbean cruising, as visibility is excellent and most approaches not difficult, many cruisers in the Caribbean use GPS with many units also linked to an on-board computer with chart plotting capabilities. Now that the prices of GPS units have dropped so dramatically, many cruisers also opt for a handheld GPS in addition to the main installation.

Autopilots

Once under way, most cruisers flick on the autopilot. It earns its keep by steering a constant course and by providing a break from the helm, particularly on the shorthanded boat. (See Chapter 5). The choice of unit will depend on the size, design and balance of the boat as well as the expected performance. The manufacturer's estimate of power consumption can be optimistic and may not always reflect usage at sea in rough conditions, which is just the time you don't want to be standing behind the wheel and would rather let Otto do the job.

Radar

Radar is not essential for Caribbean cruising but can be useful for detecting rain squalls on longer passages at night or for navigating along coasts in the dark, entering and leaving harbor at night plus plotting the distance of other shipping. Consider the location of the radar screen; it is an advantage to be able to view it from the cockpit, but easiest to use for navigation at the chart table.

Plotters

While nice to have, electronic chart plotters and programs are not essential for Caribbean cruising. One of the least expensive ways to enjoy the benefits is to run a charting software program on a laptop computer (see Chapter 9 for further comments on electronic aids).

Computers

It's no longer exceptional to find a computer on board a cruising boat. Laptops are still the most popular because of their size, portability, low power consumption and ability to work off 12 volts, sometimes through a small inverter. Those boats able to accommodate a desktop computer claim price,

John Goodwin at the nerve-centre of Speedwell of Cowes. *John built her in 1979 and has made 16 Atlantic crossings and a circumnavigation.*

hard disk size and versatility as reasons for their choice. Laptops, with their portability, give the cruiser the option of taking it ashore to access e-mail, surf the web, update software, etc. Getting computers repaired is not so easy though there is a good Compaq agent in Fort de France, Martinique. Computers are used for word processing, e-mail, weatherfax, digital image processing and many other applications.

Printer
A printer is the natural companion to the computer and the portable models win with their smaller size. It's fun to send home colorful newsletters with digital photos.

Scanners
Flat bed scanners are useful for making copies of documents before mailing and of photos to include in letters home.

Marine environment and electronics

The marine environment is hostile to most things except those naturally living in it. Electronics onboard usually have a shorter and less reliable life than their counterparts ashore. The glossy brochures advertising the range of instruments and various aids to onboard navigation seldom give the inside story of how the delicate bowels of their creations are protected from water ingress and baking heat of the tropical sun. Every effort should be made to keep salt from coming below.

Electronics fail frequently, usually without warning, at the most inopportune moment and miles from the nearest hope of repair. Know how to cope without each piece of gear. Repair agents for most marine electronics can be found on the largest islands.

The Marine Electrical and Electronics Bible by John C. Payne covers all the electronics onboard.

9

Caribbean navigation

"Ten to starboard, coral head to port . . . OK. Steady as you go!" The voice from aloft calls out the course change and, as helmsman, you obey, scanning the water ahead for the color variations that spell out the seabed contours. You know that the look-out aloft, with his Polaroid sunglasses, can see even better than you: the distinctive khaki shades that denote a reef below the water and the bluer, deeper and safe depth to one side.

Earlier, at anchor, sitting in the cockpit in the cool of the morning draining your coffee mug, you'd gazed over the turquoise shallows to the lapis blue water beyond and spotted a couple of white sails pulling nicely a few miles off. Farther still, several misty green mountains rise out of the dark blue sea, their heads pointing to the "Thomas the Tank Engine" clouds that sit, unhurried, above. The sun is already teasing golden sparkles on the water as you turn to the crew, "It looks nice out there, let's go to that island today." Welcome to Caribbean navigation.

Naturally, you then consult the chart and see that, apart from a couple of reefs that should be easy to spot as you approach under high sun, the island in question has several good bays. The guide book advises of a particularly pretty anchorage enhanced by the author's recommendation for the local eatery and bar. There's little more to be done than tidy up, weigh anchor and set sail. Navigation in the Caribbean is largely eyeball, you can judge the depth of the water by its color and with most of the islands visible from the next there is seldom the need to sail after dark.

Daytime eyeball navigation

In the Caribbean, the clarity of the water is a great help when judging depths but a good pair of Polaroid sunglasses is essential. The higher the eye, the better the definition, and any position up the mast, having regard to comfort and safety, is an advantage for the observer. Mast steps or ratlines come into their own here. The light is best between 1000 and 1500 hours with the sun behind you. With the sun ahead, or behind a cloud, in overcast or outside these times, definition can be unreliable.

Deep water appears deep blue and gets progressively paler and more turquoise as it gets shallower. Coral shows in shallow water as greeny/brown or golden brown (khaki) and rocks as darker brown. Grass and weed lack the rich brown color and appear more a neutral gray/brown. Sandy bottoms appear light golden as the water shallows; you will easily spot the patches of sand among weed where the helmsman can be guided so the anchor can be dropped.

A study of the chart will show that many small islands or rocky outcrops off a headland may be joined by a shallow sand spit or reef lying just below the surface. This might reveal itself by confused water along its margin and the look-out should always suspect any jutting point of land as having a reef, spur of rocks or sandbar beyond. A sandbar or reef just below the surface reveals itself with a thin cresting wave that moves sideways, tumbling as it goes. All crew members should practice assessing the depth and spotting the difference between coral, rock, weeds and sand.

Paper charts

Despite all the claims for computer charting, most cruisers still rely on paper charts with the useful back-up of other "black boxes." Now that the fudge factor has been removed from GPS, pinpointing your position is a fact. You must be careful, however, when using charts based on old surveys as your lat/long from GPS may not agree with what is on paper.

In the Caribbean, the most widely-used charts are Imray-Iolaire (obtainable in the Caribbean) that are specifically designed for the cruising sailor. The more recently introduced Caribbean Yachting Charts (CYC) published by Nautical Charts GmbH, available from Bluewater Books and other good chart agencies, are worth a look. For the French islands the French charts are excellent. Charts, pilots and guides are good currency but make a considerable dent in the cruising budget. Paper charts need plenty of space and it's a good idea to keep a catalog of those you have so that, should a swapping opportunity come up, you can see at a glance what you might be short of or no longer need. At many popular cruising centers cruising paperware is readily bought, sold, bartered, borrowed, swapped and photocopied. Along with all this chart barter comes a wealth of experience and information that cruisers readily swap with each other. A request from another cruiser who has visited those places you have in mind is usually a cue for a profitable hour or so of first-hand data exchange that is often more detailed

Running down Drake Channel, BVI – one of the easiest island groups to cruise. Standing on the bow, you get a unique view with only the rush of the bow wave for company.

and current than the printed guide. Most Caribbean chandlers carry charts.

Be aware that most charts are copyrighted. It is illegal to photocopy any but the US DMA charts. High quality photocopies of DMA charts can be obtained from Tides End Ltd. (see Appendix 2).

GPS

There will be occasions when you want to make a longer trip, to leap-frog several islands. You then plan a passage with one or several overnights and fall back on standard navigation techniques.

Since the advent of GPS, conning the boat safely has become easier and no one would doubt the usefulness of the other electronic aids to navigation mentioned below.

With the improvement in miniaturization and increased sales bringing the price down each season, many boats now carry a handheld GPS as a back-up to the hard wired boxes. This is not quite as excessive as it might appear for should you ever find yourself ashore on a pitch dark night, a handheld GPS for the shore party guarantees a safe return to the mother ship if visibility fails (after remembering to record the ship's position as the home waypoint).

Radar

As mentioned in the previous chapter, radar might seem unnecessary in the Caribbean but on inter-island night passages it is useful for checking the distance of approaching vessels and the distance off the coast. Radar is also useful on a dark night when sailing eastward along the north shores off Venezuela to Trinidad (see Chapter 20).

Electronic charts, navigation programs

The variety of electronic chart plotters and computer navigation programs on the market increases each year and we have found our electronic charting software, run on a laptop, very useful as an adjunct to the paper chart, especially when planning or navigating through areas with many small islands and narrow passages. Plotters are not essential to navigating in the Caribbean, just nice to have.

Cruising guides

Cruising guides are the bibles of the Caribbean cruiser and provide a wealth of information to aid the best and safest enjoyment of the islands that would take years for you to amass. Updated regularly, these guides with their chartlets and color photos will answer nearly all questions of where to go and how to get there, along with where to eat and other essential facts such as locating Customs, fuel, marine services and groceries. The cruising guides issued by Cruising Guide Publications (Nancy and Simon Scott, Chris Doyle and Bruce Van Sant) are excellent and guides issued by Don Street include much pilotage information (see Further Reading).

10

Maintenance

Most full time cruisers reckon that up to 50 per cent of their cruising budget goes on maintenance. The Jobs to Do list seems always full of jobs that really should be done Right Now. Prioritizing becomes an art. Unless your budget allows you to pull in to the nearest marina and employ help every time something goes down, you will need to know quite a bit about your boat's systems and how to keep them happy.

When gear breaks down unexpectedly, you need to be carrying the correct spares or the local currency to pay for services at your location, as the job may well occur in a place where you didn't plan to spend much money.

Keep an accurate log of routine jobs, oil changes, battery top-ups, for it may surprise you how quickly the days pass. The term "week-end" becomes meaningless without the regular pattern of shore life.

Depending on the efficacy of your bottom paint (anti-fouling), you will probably be hauling the boat annually as Caribbean barnacles are in a class by themselves and fouling is heavy. Most bottom paints are copper based. Tin based paints, for steel and aluminum vessels, are currently available but not in the USVI.

Anchors and chains rust, brass fittings tarnish, chrome deteriorates and some stainless steel isn't. If your anchor or chain is sound but showing wear, regalvanizing can sometimes be done in Venezuela. Re-brassing and chroming is available in Trinidad but as the process is done in periodic batches you should allow enough time to catch the cycle.

Tropical conditions are harder on standing rigging and regular checks should be made; swaged terminals being the worst culprits. Greasing the stainless fixings with anhydrous lanolin helps to lessen corrosion.

Build in extra time at haul-out aiming to get all jobs done together. A hauled boat gets very hot in the tropics. Renting an air-conditioning unit, if available, to fit over a hatch will make life bearable when working below (see Chapter 5).

Fouling

Barnacles will start to grow on chain and line after only a few days in the water. Some anchorages are notoriously bad, such as Chaguaramas, Trinidad, or Simpson Bay Lagoon, Sint Maarten. If anchored for more than a few days raise the chain for about 12–15 feet and clean off the budding barnacles with a stiff brush. Left any longer, the growth becomes so well established that you'll be faced with the disagreeable task of poking each link clean with metal tools. The worst growth is near the surface so the job does not require resetting the anchor. Wear sailing boots and gloves when cleaning barnacles off chain as the vicious little cuts inflicted by barnacle shards infect quickly (see Chapter 17).

Weed grows quickly on the sunlight band at water level and with the boat always lying head to the east, the starboard side will have the best harvest. Given the warm clear water, it's not a hardship to spend an hour or two periodically going around the waterline with a scraper.

Propellers

Props are notoriously difficult to keep clean; rotation speed soon spins off anti-fouling paint. Barnacles and other hard marine growth may penetrate the cutless bearing and grow around grooves. When the shaft first turns after a spell of inactivity, the hard calcium acts like sandpaper on the metal. If you stay at an anchorage for more than 4–5 days, start the engine and run the boat gently forward and astern to keep the growth down. Even the smallest amount of growth on the propeller will cause cavitation and loss of drive. Dive on the propeller periodically and scrape burgeoning growth with a flat metal scraper. Wear diving gloves to protect hands when scraping the hull and prop.

Haul-out

The choice of places to haul out in the Caribbean increases each year. Where to go is largely a matter of which place takes your fancy, how much work needs doing, the type of jobs and whether you want contract labor, do-it-yourself or leave the boat stored while you travel. Most large boatyards have well-stocked chandlers on site or close by plus other services. Budget Marine and Island Water World have chandlers in the larger islands. Some islands are more convenient for importing duty-free parts, such as Trinidad and Sint Maarten/St. Martin or the US Virgins for parts from the United States.

Listed below are a few of the most popular places for haul-out and servicing but it is by no means exclusive and study of the cruising guides will give a much fuller idea of what's currently on offer for the cruiser. Several major charter companies operate large fleets from various locations throughout the Caribbean, and they all need reliable marine services; you can often use the same service for your own problems. Consulting other cruisers can also give you up-to-date information of good service experiences.

US Virgin Islands
In the USVI, Haulover Marine in Crown Bay and Independent Boat Yard near Red Hook, both on St. Thomas, provide service yards with all facilities. Obtaining parts from the States is a breeze.

British Virgin Islands
Tortola and Virgin Gorda offer good facilities for haul-out, servicing and storage. Add to this, super cruising, reasonably priced food stores, chandlery and good travel links to the US and Europe, and you have an attractive package.

Sint Maarten/St. Martin
This is a very popular place for getting work done and do-it-yourself. Many service facilities are located around Simpson Bay Lagoon including sail making, rigging, refrigeration, electronic and engine repairs. Land-locked, with two drawbridge entrances opening to the sea, the lagoon offers good shelter and tranquil waters for getting on with those do-it-yourself jobs and many cruisers spend some time here enjoying the community atmosphere.

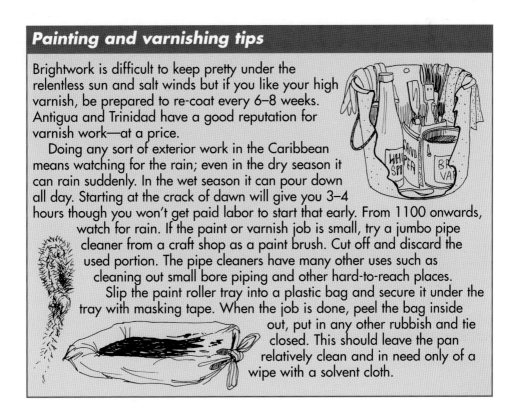

Painting and varnishing tips

Brightwork is difficult to keep pretty under the relentless sun and salt winds but if you like your high varnish, be prepared to re-coat every 6–8 weeks. Antigua and Trinidad have a good reputation for varnish work—at a price.

Doing any sort of exterior work in the Caribbean means watching for the rain; even in the dry season it can rain suddenly. In the wet season it can pour down all day. Starting at the crack of dawn will give you 3–4 hours though you won't get paid labor to start that early. From 1100 onwards, watch for rain. If the paint or varnish job is small, try a jumbo pipe cleaner from a craft shop as a paint brush. Cut off and discard the used portion. The pipe cleaners have many other uses such as cleaning out small bore piping and other hard-to-reach places.

Slip the paint roller tray into a plastic bag and secure it under the tray with masking tape. When the job is done, peel the bag inside out, put in any other rubbish and tie closed. This should leave the pan relatively clean and in need only of a wipe with a solvent cloth.

Budget Marine and Island Water World have their main chandlers here with extensive supplies. Bobby's Marina and Boatyard in Philipsburg has a travelift. Since it is a duty-free island, there is no problem with importing parts for a yacht in transit and most service facilities are familiar with the process and will be able to help if you can supply the necessary part number and manufacturer's fax or telephone number. There is an international airport.

Antigua
Haul-out services are offered at Jolly Harbour and English Harbour. Jolly Harbour, built beside a lagoon with sea access halfway up the western shore, is a holiday complex and marina, with attendant facilities and Budget Marine. A bus service runs into St. John's with access to the airport and the other resorts on the island.

Around Falmouth Harbour are engineering services, a sail loft, electronic and refrigeration services and riggers. Antigua Slipway in English Harbour offers haul-out and chandlery, fuel and water. Antigua is relatively expensive and importing goods for the boat can be a tiresome procedure requiring trips out and back to the airport between Customs and tax office.

Guadeloupe
There are haul-out and service facilities at Pointe-à-Pitre.

Martinique
This island has a well earned reputation for good haul-out and maintenance services with a large marina and yard in Marin in the south. Supermarché Annette next door has all the French goodies you need.

St. Lucia
With its annual hosting of the ARC finish in Rodney Bay, St. Lucia is a popular place to haul-out with storage facilities and chandlery. The capital, Castries, also has a service yard with the added advantage of being close to town.

Grenada
Spice Island Marine, at the southern end of the island, is a small haul-out yard. The newer Granada Marine at St. David's Harbour in the southeast offers extensive facilities including a 70-ton travel-hoist. On Carriacou, part of Grenada, Tyrrel Bay Yacht Haul-Out is a new yard with a 50-ton hoist.

Trinidad

This is a very popular cruiser's rendezvous with extensive services. In 1994 when we first visited, there were only two small boat yards that could haul a sailing boat. Today there is a choice of more than 8 marinas, from modest to well-equipped high tech, that can cater for boats up to 150 tons.

Trinidad, with its commercial marine history going back more than 60 years, is well geared for all marine needs. Trinidadians will boast that you can get anything you want here—and it's just about true. Quickly realizing the potential business with cruising yachts, the government ruled that yachts in transit may import goods for their yachts ex duty. The process is largely hassle-free and has won for Trinidad a large slice of the annual maintenance business among itinerant yachts of all sizes. Add to this the month-long Carnival and it's not hard to understand why cruising boats have formed a large and supportive community that is difficult to leave and to which many cruisers return annually, and not just for haul-out.

Since it is below the hurricane belt, many boats head to Trinidad for the hurricane season. One disadvantage is that it can rain heavily most days during the summer and humidity is high at all times of the year. You will need to take that into account when planning any work. There are few maintenance facilities on the sister island of Tobago.

Honey Jar, just hauled, being loaded onto the transporter at Peake's yard, Chaguaramas, Trinidad. The next boat is already waiting its turn in the slip.

Venezuela

Although Venezuela is outside the area of this guide, some boats head there during the hurricane season. Boatyards at Cumana and more popularly, Puerto La Cruz, can provide most of the services usually required. A boatyard has recently opened in Margarita. Brush up on your Spanish.

11

Weather

Weather is a hot topic in the Caribbean. Though you might think that Caribbean weather only varies between hot and hotter there are significant weather patterns that need watching if you're not to be caught with your guard down. Marine SSB, Ham radio, Marine VHF, Island FM Radio and TV stations put out forecasts, mostly resourced from the US weather bureaux. Some also give valuable assessment on local weather as well as the broader picture between South and North America. Some anchorages run a daily net on VHF radio, usually in the morning. These provide useful updates on local weather forecasts as well as what's happening in the social calendar. Listening to the daily forecasts on SSB, Ham radio, VHF, FM radio and TV will provide you with a good picture of what's going on, what to expect and how and when to plan a passage.

It is important to understand the weather systems in the Caribbean as they are very different from those found in the more temperate climates further north or south.

Understanding Caribbean weather

Very simply put, the weather systems in the North Atlantic go clockwise around the ocean, with prevailing winds running west to east across the top around 40°–50° N and from east to west around 10°–20° N. The latter, known as the trade winds, are at their most settled from the end of November through to the end of May. It was these steady easterly winds of 15 to 25 knots that brought the early explorers over from Europe on their quest to find the route to the East and the lucrative spice trade. They found instead a long string of islands they called the West Indies and that we know today as the Caribbean. This handy carousel of winds allows the cruiser to a get a free ride, jumping on and off where he chooses.

A general overview of weather patterns

As already stated above, the north Atlantic weather runs clockwise while in the southern Atlantic the weather system runs anti-clockwise; the two systems are like huge gear wheels. In between these two systems, roughly between 10°S and 10°N, lies the Inter Tropical Convergence Zone or ITCZ. This is a region of squalls, rain and clear areas, moving northward in the summer and southward in the winter; it is this southern shift that leaves the door open for hurricane formation.

North of the ITCZ in the area 10°N to 20°N, the trade winds blow more or less from the east 15–25 knots, but can shift in direction from a NE through SE and change in strength. Squalls, with rain and stronger winds, also occur periodically.

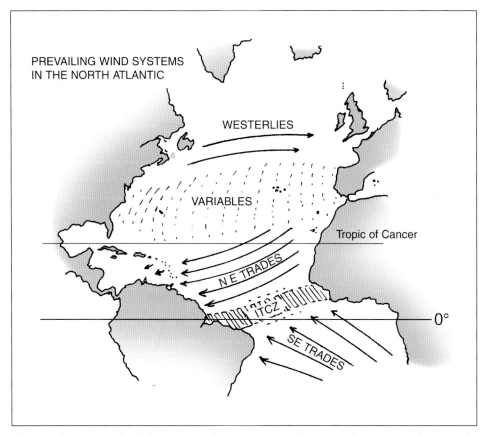

The circulating winds of the North Atlantic are steadiest near the equator forming the trade winds. The movement of the ITCZ influences the weather systems.

The winter sailing season is from November to May. Early on there is a tendency for the winds to be more north of east. As the season progresses the winds tend to be less strong, 15–20 knots, and come more from the east, sometimes with a touch of south. This seasonal north/south tendency can be used to good effect when traveling up or down the island chain. If there is a large high pressure system (Bermuda High) north of the Caribbean this may also bring an increased pressure gradient across the Caribbean, resulting in stronger trade winds of 20–25 knots. This can produce a strong easterly or northeasterly swell.

Frontal systems moving southeast off the U.S. East Coast will often stall north of the Caribbean with the southwestern end of the front near Puerto Rico. These fronts can affect the weather in the Leewards, especially the Virgin Islands.

Large low pressure systems moving across the North Atlantic during the winter can create large swells which travel down to the Caribbean. North-facing anchorages should be avoided during times of these high swell conditions as the 10- to 12-foot seas can make some anchorages untenable. Wave heights in the Caribbean can be anywhere between 2 to 12 feet depending on local and distant weather conditions.

Pressure systems over the South American mainland, atmospheric moisture levels and upper level systems all have their part to play in affecting Caribbean weather. Listening to local weather forecasts will help the Caribbean cruiser plan accordingly.

Barometric pressure

In northern temperate latitudes (roughly between 23° N and 66° N) traveling weather systems cause the barometric pressure to fluctuate in large, rapid and irregular amounts. In the tropics, however, there is little day-to-day change but within the day there is a regular 12-hour swing. The lows occur at around 0400 hours and 1600 and the highs at around 1000 and 2200 hours. At the equator this twice-daily change is an average of 3 millibars (mb), decreasing with latitude to 2.5 mb at 30°N and 1.7mb at 35°N. In the Caribbean the average is 3 mb. These diurnal variations in barometric pressure must be taken into account when making or reading a forecast. Any halt in the diurnal range might mean the advent of a tropical revolving storm (TRS). To be of any value barometric readings should be taken at the same time each day, preferably at around 0630 as this is the approximate mean. Synoptic charts give a good indication of pressure gradients and expected winds in the Caribbean.

Tropical waves

Tropical waves are troughs of low pressure, lying roughly on a north/south axis, that come off the coast of Africa and move westward at 10–15 knots. They do not rotate but they do contain wind shifts. Ahead of the wave, the wind will be from the northeast while behind the wave the wind will be from the southeast. This shift in wind direction with a tropical wave can be useful when making passages up and down the island chain. By themselves, tropical waves contain no threat, as long as they don't rotate, though they may bring clouds or squalls.

Hurricanes

Tropical revolving storm (TRS) is a term covering typhoons in the North Pacific, cyclones in the Indian Ocean and hurricanes in the Caribbean. Blowing with ungovernable fury, the high winds of a TRS whip up mountainous seas with an unbounded violence bent on destroying all in its path.

The following information relates to hurricanes occurring in the Caribbean region; details about TRSs in other parts of the world will vary from those given here.

The hurricane season in the Caribbean is considered to run from the beginning of June to the end of November, with the worst months being August, September and October. During the season, if a tropical wave develops an anti-clockwise rotation it becomes a tropical depression with the ability to gain higher wind speeds, turning into a tropical storm; whence it will be given a name, for it has the potential to become a hurricane.

If an upper level trough develops over the low level trough (tropical wave) the two can become as one, like a spinning cylinder. The winds pull the warm moist air (the system's fuel) into the center at sea level and funnel it up the chimney. The water vapor forms a deep ring of clouds, like a giant doughnut, in the typical inward moving pinwheel. The system feeds upon itself, winding up to higher and higher speeds and traveling in a curved line roughly in a northwesterly direction and at a fairly constant speed of about 15 knots. This, at least, gives the chance to predict fairly accurately when the bad weather will arrive. The winds will also generate a swell, traveling faster than the hurricane and preceding it, sometimes by hundreds of miles.

Such are the increasing demands for fuel that winds can be drawn from hundreds of miles away, being sucked into the center at ever increasing speeds. Winds of well over 100 knots are not uncommon. The diameter of

A boat yard in St. Martin after a recent hurricane. It caused a domino effect as the wind blew the boats on top of each other; many were deemed beyond repair and still lie as a silent reminder.

a tropical revolving storm can be from 50 miles to as much as 1000 miles but rarely exceeds 600 miles. In the center of the cylinder the air is eerily quiet–the eye of the hurricane–while the seas remain monstrous. The eye can be up to 40 miles wide. As the system moves, the eye moves with it and where the winds will have been from one direction ahead of the hurricane, they will shift to the opposite direction as the eye passes. Wind speeds vary over the circumference.

Draw a line through the middle of the hurricane along its track. The wind speed in the right hand quadrant will be augmented by the speed at which the hurricane is traveling, thus the strongest winds occur on the right hand semicircle. This is not the side to be as the winds will be trying to pull the ship into the center. The lefthand or navigable semi-circle gives the ship the chance to sail away from the center by keeping the wind on the starboard quarter.

The winds can only build and sustain high speeds over water, for much of the energy is derived from the latent heat released by the condensation of water vapor. This accounts for the occurrence of hurricanes in the western part of the Atlantic Ocean and Caribbean Sea where the winds have traveled a long way over warm seas. Once over land, the winds tend to dissipate due to the higher friction and lower humidity. For further reading on hurricanes in the Caribbean see *The Sailor's Weather Guide*, Second Edition, by Jeff Markell.

Sources of Caribbean weather data

Most marine weather forecast data and synoptic charts for the Caribbean are provided by the US National Weather Service, Marine Prediction Center and the Tropical Prediction Center, Miami.

Weather forecasts are broadcast on a regular schedule by United States Coast Guard station NMN, Chesapeake. The latest schedule can be obtained from *Admiralty List of Radio Signals*, NP283(2), HMSO.

Synoptic charts and satellite images are available by weather fax from the United States Coast Guard stations NMG, New Orleans and NMF, Boston. For station frequencies and schedules, refer to *Admiralty List of Radio Signals*, NP283(2), HMSO.

Useful websites

Station frequencies and schedules
http:// weather.noaa.gov/pub/fax/hfgulf.txt
http:// weather.noaa.gov/pub/fax/hfmarsh.txt

Useful radiofax information can be found at the web site
www.nws.noaa.gov/om/marine/radiofax.htm

Synoptic charts and satellite images transmitted by USCG stations NMF and NMG are also available on the Internet.
   At the time of writing, synoptic charts for NMG are available at
http:// weather.noaa.gov/fax/gulf.shtml and for NMF at
http:// weather.noaa.gov/fax/marsh.shtml

Satellite images can be found at www.goes.noaa.gov and for unclassified US Navy weather images visit www.nlmoc.navy.mil/home1.shtml

Hurricane information can be obtained from the National Hurricane Center website. Visit www.nhc.noaa.gov/

Data input from the Caribbean region for the US forecasts is limited and, as a result, local weather conditions may not agree exactly with the forecast from the NWS which covers a broad area. Because of this, local forecasters in the Caribbean region spend considerable time and effort in analyzing data from the US weather services and study the latest satellite images and interpret the data to the benefit of the cruising community.

At the time of writing, weather observations and forecasts for the Caribbean region are given on the Amateur Radio Caribbean Emergency and Weather Net on 7162 kHz LSB at 0630 hrs, and on the Amateur Radio Caribbean Net on 7241 kHz LSB at approximately 0715 hrs.

David Jones operates the Caribbean Weather Centre in Tortola, British Virgin Islands, and gives a general synopsis followed by detailed weather to vessels sponsoring his service (see Chapter 18). His book, *Caribbean Weather*, gives a clear explanation of the weather systems.

Virgin Islands Radio, WAH, broadcasts weather for Puerto Rico and the Virgin Islands on ITU channel 401–4357 kHz and VHF channel 85 at 0600, 1800 and 2200 and on channel 85 only at 0800 and 2000 hrs local. Virgin Islands Radio also transmits weather continuously on weather channel WX3.

Herb Hilgenberg is another name known to experienced cruisers. Herb runs a weather service covering the North Atlantic and his services are used by many sailors heading for North America or back to Europe at the end of the season. If you are considering your choice of movements at the end of the season you will find details of his net in Chapter 20.

In some islands, TV stations give local weather including satellite images. Radio stations may give local weather also. Local marine and VHF radio nets often relay weather forecasts in their areas. Visitors to the Caribbean should check the latest situation with the appropriate nets and other providers of information.

Navtex broadcasts

Storm warnings, synopses and forecasts for the East Caribbean are broadcast by Navtex by US Coast Guard station NMR in Puerto Rico, identification character [R].

12

Anchoring & mooring

Having safely navigated your way to your chosen island, the job's not yet done. Securing the boat to land, be it under water or above is a basic skill with different facets depending on location. In the Caribbean there are an increasing number of moorings for rent but most cruisers choose to lie to their own tackle, when they can find a space. It's cheaper, plus there is the comfort of knowing your own gear rather than risking the condition of a strange mooring; 200 feet (65 meters) of chain is an adequate amount to carry for most anchorages and wind conditions in the Caribbean. Winds in the Caribbean are usually 15–25 knots; in gusts and squalls winds of up to 30 knots are not unusual and some anchorages can get quite uncomfortable.

When seeking to anchor in deserted bays, a study of the chart plus the latest weather forecast will dictate where the skipper places the ship for the best lie to the wind and protection from any swells or predicted bad weather.

In the more popular anchorages, the same research is necessary but now the lie of other craft must be taken into account. Finding a spot that gives safe and decent clearance from other boats is paramount. In open anchorages such as the Tobago Cays, where the trade wind is unimpeded from the east, all yachts lie straight downwind and the only precaution is to spot those boats that have a tendency to sail around their anchor. Motor boats tend to do this more than sail boats but a short cruise around will show the culprits and an allowance must be made for their movements.

Anchorages with steep-to hills behind are prone to down drafts and you must allow for a certain amount of gusting and swinging. This would be simple enough if everyone lay to chain but a number of boats use rope and consequently make a larger swing. It is common in the smaller bays to take a line (usually the stern) to the shore and make fast to a palm tree or rock. In Peter Island, in the British Virgin Islands, for example, where the hills cause the winds to circle, it is common to see a "daisy chain" of boats all with their anchors to the center and stern lines to the shore.

Cranking a manual windlass can be slow and tiring, particularly if you have to re-set under difficult conditions.

Anchoring technique

Given the usual cruising crew of one man and one woman, many couples find that the woman is better on the helm while the skipper does the fore-deck work and is responsible for assuring a secure set. While tidal swing is negligible, there can be a current which may not harmonize with the wind direction, causing boats to lie in different directions.

Most bottoms are sandy, there are some anchorages with eel grass or weed making them notoriously unyielding. Some anchors (CQR in particular) don't like weed but often a short sortie around such an anchorage will show, by the color of the water, a sandy patch just big enough for the anchor to dig in. When the operation is complete the reward is to have a dive over the side with mask and snorkel and get a visual check on the set of the anchor. (For more on depth by water color, see Chapter 9.)

Work out some non-vocal signals between helm and bow that avoid raised voices, for engine and wind noise can mangle speech. Agree on what needs to be done before starting the maneuver. You can be sure of an audience when you enter or leave an anchorage and it's nice to complete the trick in a quiet, seamanlike manner without recourse to histrionics. You've seen it happen.

As in any anchorage, the boat after you is obliged to move if there is conflict over swinging room. As feathers are easily ruffled in these situations, phrases such as "I'm not very happy with your position," will get your message across and save face all round rather than more combative expressions. Just sitting in the cockpit and studying *Bad Dog* as it swings will often bring results without a word spoken. Most skippers accept that having arrived last they must defer to others if necessary.

As gusts and squalls are unpredictable, a rope snubber will take the strain off the windlass.

Anchor types

CQR
Delta
Fortress
Bruce

CQR
A very popular type in the Caribbean, good in most bottom conditions but can be difficult setting in eel grass or weed.
Delta
This is an increasingly popular anchor. Similar to a CQR but without the moving head.
Bruce
Another popular bower anchor, but in loose, dead coral it has a nasty habit of grabbing a coral boulder that prevents it from setting.
Danforth
This is a good anchor in sand but it can hook coral boulders like the Bruce.

Fortress
Similar to a Danforth but lighter and easier to handle. Good as a second anchor in doubtful conditions. A useful anchor to deploy from the dinghy because of its light weight.
Fisherman
This anchor is not often seen except on traditional and fishing craft.

A handy tip is to paint the anchor and stock white. It is easier to spot on the bottom when you snorkel to check the set. Galvanized anchors can look a lot like dead coral boulders at depth.

Ground tackle

Anchors come in all types and sizes; it is not possible to list them all. Listed below are some of the more popular types in no particular order of merit. Don't economize; Caribbean winds can gust over 30 knots without warning. Fit one size larger than specified as your bower, fitted with appropriate chain calibrated for your windlass. On *Honey Jar* we carried four anchors of various sizes, using each of them at various times and have used them all at once on occasions. We know of boats that carry more.

Scope

This is your life. The old rule of 3 to 1 for chain is generally not enough in the Caribbean; 4 to 1 is better depending on conditions, the available room in the anchorage, bottom type, anchor weight and chain size. Unless it is just for lunch, you would seldom lie to less than 4 or 5 to 1, if in doubt more. When calculating depth include the additional height from water to stemhead. In greater depth, more catenary means less snatch. In shallow water more scope is required as there is little or no catenary from chain.

It is worth considering the pros and cons of chain versus rope.

Chain

Pros: Nothing like it for the feel-good factor. Strong and resistant to abrasion, especially in coral and sand. The weight of chain gives a catenary which takes up the shock of gusts when anchored in deeper water. It comes up clean from the sandy seabed.
Cons: Heavy, expensive (but don't economize on quality or condition), goes rusty more quickly with constant use than with holiday sailing. Caribbean sand is abrasive and Trinidadian mud is corrosive.

Rode

Pros: Easier and lighter to handle, particularly from the dinghy if you're setting or retrieving a second hook. It has good stretch and takes up snatch from gusty winds. It is cheaper than chain, lighter to stow and doesn't rust.
Cons: Chafes easily on coral. Holds mud, which can work into the fibers. Lying to rope means setting a greater scope (approximately 7:1).

Snatch

Cruising boats spend a lot of time at anchor and Caribbean anchorages can have quite a swell. A snubber or bridle made of nylon rope (multi-plait gives plenty of stretch) will take the strain off the windlass and lessen snatch. Allow sufficient length to run at least 10 feet (3 meters) from the securing points on the foredeck. Some consider that the use of a galvanized hook puts a strain on the links and prefer to use a rolling hitch and spliced loop at the other end over the sampson post. Thread the rope through a short piece of clear plastic water pipe to act as a chafe guard at the point where the line comes in contact with the boat, be it bow roller, hawse hole or toerail cleat. (Secure the pipe to the snubber with light line.)

Using a springy nylon snubber with a rolling hitch is cheap, works well and doesn't distress chain.

Windlass

On all but the smallest boats, raising chain and anchor aboard by hand on a frequent basis can be very hard work, especially in winds from 15–25 knots. A windlass is a useful investment. A hand windlass makes the task easier but is very slow, especially if the anchor doesn't take the first time and you have to raise all the tackle then reset it several times. Our record in the Caribbean was 10 times with our CQR into a grass bottom and that was hard work even with a powered windlass.

An electric windlass is a hefty investment but worth every penny for it saves more backs from strain than it breaks with its price. Foot controls need to be in a place where they won't be activated accidentally as it's usual to leave the breaker switch in the ON position for instant use. Through-deck fittings need to be well bedded in compound to stop water getting to the contacts below and it's worth carrying a spare switch (or two) as they are prone to fail. Remote control is handy, for it's often necessary to stand right at the stemhead to check the lay of the chain, spot coral heads and direct the helm. In the event of power failure you need to be able to operate the windlass manually.

Many boats, starting out with a manual windlass or none at all, often add an electric windlass as a priority once cruising. An electric windlass encourages re-anchoring in difficult holding to get a good fix.

If you don't think you need a windlass, practice weighing anchor in a force 5–6 (average trade wind) and you might change your mind.

Chain for the windlass

Make sure you know the size of chain suited to your windlass. Chain is available in three types: *Proof coil* with long links and generally unsuited to windlasses; *BBB*, which is calibrated to suit most windlasses, and *High Test* which is also suited to windlasses but the links are slightly longer than BBB.

The life of chain in constant use in the Caribbean might be no more than three or four years.

Moorings

The rise in yachting tourism in the Caribbean has seen the increase in rental moorings on the premise that anchors destroy the coral. This is doubtful, for no prudent sailor would choose to anchor on coral and risk the possibility of an insecure set, or snagging and losing his tackle. Nevertheless, the preservation of coral is a concern and cruisers should aim to anchor with minimal disturbance to the environment.

Moorings are always charged for (except in St. John National Park, USVI, see below). However, there may be some incentive such as those laid by restaurants or shops who will make a discount for meals or items bought. Picking up any mooring deems you liable for payment.

Some anchorages are now so full of moorings as to restrict anchoring to the outer fringes. Trellis Bay on Beef Island in the BVIs is a favorite last stop as the tiny airport is just a stone's throw from the beach but there are so many moorings now that anchoring is limited. For all that, it's worth a visit if only to have dinner at The Last Resort, a restaurant on the little cay in the center of the bay and listen to the cabaret (à la Noel Coward), complete with resident donkey looking on through the window.

Certain protected areas are designated as marine parks and use of a mooring is mandatory. At The Baths, Virgin Gorda, BVIs, anchoring is forbidden but it is a stunning location; go early to secure a mooring but be aware that it can get uncomfortable in a northeast swell.

In St. John National Park, USVI, anchoring is forbidden and park moorings must be used. Currently, these moorings are free but fees may be introduced. Check with the Park Services Department in their building opposite the Customs office in Cruz Bay, St. John. Here you can pick up brochures with a moorings' map as well as other interesting information about the island and park.

Some moorings can be booked in advance by phone. The Cut at the south end of St. Vincent is an attractive place to stop, and handy for the airport if you are meeting or dropping off visitors or crew. A mooring is best reserved here as it is a popular spot and with a flight schedule you'll want to be sure of a place to come ashore for a taxi.

13

Chores & stores

Chores

One of the most frequently asked questions of cruisers is "So what do you actually *do* with all that leisure time?" In reality, there isn't all that much leisure time. Chores cannot be avoided no matter where you live. Even the humblest crofter must spend part of the day gathering fuel, sweeping the floor, tending the livestock and ensuring the larder holds sufficient food to last till the next foray before he attends to the leak in the roof, the hinge on the door or the wheel on the wagon. So it is with the cruising boat; cruising isn't one long holiday. Systems must be kept running smoothly and the boat maintained to a decent standard so as not to give the impression of being a boat bum. Apart from the unrelenting task of keeping the ship clean and tidy, the four regular chores are: fuel, water, food and laundry. Maintenance is another story and gets a chapter to itself.

Housework doesn't go away on a boat. Hair and dust will lie on all surfaces or collect in fluff bunnies. Everything that can fall into the bilge will try to do so, the smaller the better. Wiping surfaces and floors with a damp cloth helps to keep the worst down but if your power resources will cope, invest in a small domestic vacuum cleaner. Power it via a generator or with an inverter while the engine is running for battery charging. Discard the floor head and use the dusting brush instead for floors, etc, and bring a spare one.

A 12-volt car vacuum type is not worth the price. It is too high a drain on the battery to run for longer than a few minutes and is just adequate for dusting. On the other hand a cordless Dust Buster handheld mini-vacuum, charged from an inverter, is good for those quick clean ups after jobs that leave wood or metal shavings, sewing threads, or when the grill pan spills toast crumbs on the floor. All these bits need herding away from the bilge or they could block the strum box. Hair is the worst culprit.

Laundry

There is seldom difficulty getting laundry done in the Caribbean and in most places you will find a Laundromat or local women who will do it for you.

Getting to a Laundromat can involve a walk and a cart comes in useful here, as laundry is likely to have built up to several bags by the time you reach a convenient anchorage. Surprisingly, in the Caribbean, most Laundromats have tumble dryers, despite the sun and wind that would be welcomed on an English Monday. It may seem madness to use a tumble dryer in the tropics but you come back with clean, dry, folded laundry that goes straight into the locker.

In some anchorages, local women will collect your laundry and return it washed, dried and folded. This is convenient but not always the cheapest way and your laundry may go in with other loads. Nearly all washing machines in the Caribbean are American, the old fashioned top-loading, paddle-agitator type and detergents are similar to what you're used to. The washing cycle is fast, about 25 minutes, but the single rinsing dulls clothes after a while.

Hand washing is fine if you can spare enough ship's water for a proper job, have wrists strong enough to wring and don't mind the chore of pegging it out, away from salty rigging and watching the sky for the next shower or seeing it fly away in a squall.

With the easy access to Laundromats, hand washing seems hardly worth the bother. Make the laundry part of a trip ashore, have a quiet read or write letters. Laundromats tend to be social places and you'll probably find other cruisers to swap yarns or books. This is also a good place to learn about local facilities and get help on any boat-related problems.

Don't even think about washing laundry in sea water; you'll use even more precious fresh water trying to rinse the salt out. The slightest hint of salt and your dried washing will come out of the locker smelling of mildew.

Tanking up

Fuel

Diesel is readily available throughout the Caribbean and the quality fairly reliable. Some cruisers carry Baja fuel filters (available from West Marine), but these are cumbersome, need special stowage and slow the filling rate considerably. They do, however, guarantee pristine fuel. Another option is to fit at least two in-line filters as well as having a drain or sump facility at the bottom of the fuel tank to remove water. Keeping the tanks topped up helps to reduce condensation though this is not such a problem in the tropics. Condensation can still form on cooler nights and the less air in the tank, the less condensation can form. It's a good idea to keep the tanks brimmed, just in case you need to make a quick get-away.

In St. Martin/Sint Maarten and other French islands, diesel is called gasoil.

Gasoline and kerosene are also available but you may carry these in smaller quantities in jerry cans.

Always enquire if the filler has any quirks. Some blow back easily, others leak, or drip, the auto shut-off doesn't work or the lock doesn't stay on unless held. In any case never leave the filler unattended.

Water

Watermakers are now becoming a common item on cruising boats but they are power hungry, particularly at each start-up and require careful maintenance to prevent expensive membrane replacements. Making water aboard is seldom cheaper than buying (there is no free water in the Caribbean), but it does ensure you an independent source of pure water which extends your time between shore station stops.

All the islands have potable water, the mountainous ones from their own catchment and the lower ones from desalinators. We have never found it necessary to dose the tank with chlorine nor drink only bottled water (available in supermarkets). Water on the dock, however, will have been treated and while potable has a taste that you might not want in your drinks; an in-line filter to the drinking water tap makes for better-tasting coffee or tea. The average cost for dockside water is 5–6 cents per liter (in 2001) but can be more in those islands that have to import water.

It rains a lot in the Caribbean and you can fill your tank with this bounty if you have a means of catching it. An awning can be fashioned in such a way as to collect the rain and funnel it into the tanks direct or into some suitable vessel where, covered, it will be adequate for cooking and washing. It is best to let a certain amount run off first to rinse away accumulated salt and dust, then run it through a muslin filter into the tanks.

If you have clean, painted decks, after an initial rinse, you can dam the flow behind the filler and let the accumulated water run into the tank. It's not a good idea to try this with teak decks for they are never entirely free of salt, dirt or the fine gray fibers of the wood.

Carrying enough pure water for all needs is one of the top priorities on a cruising boat. How much you need depends on your life style and discipline. Without a water maker you are dependent on your tankage and some sort of restraint is required between fill-ups. Pressure water systems inevitably use more water than manual pumping.

A gallon water bottle, with the bottom cut off and a water-pipe neck extension, makes a wide funnel for catching rain. Hang a muslin filter from rim. A wooden skewer pushed horizontally through the pipe stops it from falling into the tank.

Shopping

Leaving for a cruise begs the question "What to take and what to leave behind?" When it comes to food, most of us have our favorites: things we like to eat, are used to or require for dietary needs. Without prior knowledge of what's available at your destination, the impulse can be to take just about everything you can think of.

Arguably, some of the best places to shop are the French islands with Super Marché Annette in Marin, Martinique, being a favorite choice with many cruisers for stocking up on wine, cheese and other desirable French goodies. A bus from Fort de France to Hyper-U (ask for Eeeper-oo) will bring you to an enormous complex with the biggest hypermarket in the islands, plus many other shops and stores. St. Martin/Sint Maarten boasts large supermarkets on the French and the Dutch side with specialties from both countries. The US and British Virgin Islands are also rated highly for groceries, fruit and vegetables, while Trinidad is hard to beat with fruit and vegetables available all through the year.

Shops with barely 100 square feet of floor space will call themselves a supermarket but you might prefer to seek out a larger, air-conditioned shop. That is not to say the tiny local store is unsafe. I have noted the undeniable aroma of Rat in an air-conditioned shop in a classy resort. Let your eyes and nose be your guide.

Everything you buy ashore will eventually have to be carried back to the dinghy, even if you use a local bus. The tiniest shop will give you plastic bags but it's worth considering a folding cart with a folding basket for serious forays on foot. The cart will come in useful for carrying fuel, cans, propane bottles and water containers also, as these supplies are not always on the dockside. Carts aren't always accepted on buses.

When we left Devon bound for the Canaries and our Atlantic crossing, I filled every available space with basics: rice, pasta, oats, flour, sugar, tea and coffee. Three years later we were still eating English pasta shells, a little past their best. (It was heartening to read that Linda Dashew, an experienced sailor, did the same thing). All the above basics and more are readily available in the Caribbean plus lots of exotic foods you'll have fun trying.

In some local bookshops you will find several excellent cookbooks written for cruisers new to Caribbean cuisine. My own book, *Reluctant Cook*, is aimed at the less-than-enthusiastic cruising cook with simple and easy recipes, along with some cartoons to lighten things up a little.

Cruising shopping means buying items when you find them as supplies can be sporadic, particularly of imported goods. When you see an item you need, buy it—or even buy several as you don't know when or where you'll find them again. Though the islands are poor, people seldom starve, for with the tropical climate and fertile soil there's always something edible sprouting from the ground or falling off a branch.

Market produce

Shopping at the local markets is fun and most stall holders will give you tips on preparing an unfamiliar item. The local fruit and vegetables are flavorful, though you will have to accept the blemishes along with the bounty. Fruit and vegetable markets and small stores are seldom refrigerated so your purchases will last longer. Imported produce tends to be second grade, not suited for the home market but just as nutritious. Potatoes, sometimes called Irish potatoes to distinguish them from sweet potatoes and yams, are available as are carrots but these are usually imported. Salad greens don't grow well in the tropics, developing too quickly to form a good heart; the lettuces you do find will be small and open except in Trinidad where lettuce is good and leafy. You will find imported Iceberg lettuce but it's usually second grade and you'll need to pick them over carefully to choose the least bruised. Iceberg and white cabbage both keep well and are best peeled leaf by leaf as cut edges quickly brown. In the US and British Virgin Islands, the larger supermarkets carry a wider range of imported salad greens.

Carrots, mostly imports, tend to go slimy quickly unless refrigerated. Wrapping individually in paper and laying in a cool locker works quite well but it's a tiresome routine. You will find tomatoes and cucumbers, both local and imported. Celery is the local spindly kind and expensive. Imported celery is available in some larger supermarkets.

Potatoes keep well in a cool locker, check and knock off sprouts daily to stop dehydration. Yams and sweet potatoes are delicious; peel after cooking whole in the oven, microwave or pressure cooker, then scoop out the flesh and serve with butter, salt and pepper. Cooking sweet potatoes whole will prevent the flesh turning gray, peel then mash with plenty of milk, butter and seasoning; they have a nutty taste. Other locally grown root vegetables keep well.

Bananas, cheap and delicious, are likely to be local or certainly Caribbean, eaten raw or cooked in many different sweet and savory recipes. Plantains look like large pointy bananas but must be cooked. Sliced and fried, they are delicious with meat, especially bacon. Other vegetables such as broccoli and beans are imported though you may find the local very long bean in some markets. Christophene is like a hard green pear: peel and slice the flesh from around the large pit, sprinkle with salt, chill and eat raw or chop and boil as a vegetable. Locally grown pineapple is sweeter than canned and the juice is good as a meat tenderizer in a marinade.

It may look quaintly nautical to hang the fruit on deck but the salt atmosphere and bright light will ripen it all too quickly. That is if the fruit bats haven't eaten it the night before and fouled your cockpit with their putrid droppings.

Meat and fish

Meat is rated as good to excellent. Most is imported from the US; buying from larger, air-conditioned stores where the turnover is high, usually gives you a better selection. Chicken is usually frozen, from the US, likewise lamb. You will find local beef on some of the larger islands plus goat, and cow heel; the former is prepared as a stew and the latter made into a tasty soup. A wide variety of fresh fish, including some you might not know, can be bought from local markets and stalls; all make good eating.

Food to store

Flour for baking is widely available but you will seldom find strong (durum) wheat flour for bread and will have to be content with the pastry grade. Wrapped sliced white or wholewheat bread, and rolls for hot-dogs, are made to the American recipe with more sugar; it is drier and crumblier than English bread. It may be locally baked or imported. Cakes, pies, pastries and biscuits are usually baked locally. Cookies and crackers are usually imported from the US.

Many cruisers do a lot of home baking. If you're not an enthusiastic cook you might find Bisquick a life saver; most big stores have it (send for the recipe book). The purist cook may shudder at such low-down cheating but we reluctant cooks grab at anything to get us out of a hole. Basically a pastry mix, it readily adapts itself to all sorts of dishes, sweet and savory and there are many quick and tasty recipes to be made from the contents of that yellow box. The popular breakfast cereals are available but pricey, except for oatmeal; fruit and home-made muesli makes a cheaper breakfast.

You're in the land of sugar, white and various shades of brown, plentiful and cheap. The sugar islands are also the spice islands and you'll find more spices than you'll know what to do with.

Canned foods (fruit, vegetables, meat and fish) are plentiful as well as cooking sauces, both local and imported. Dried foods, such as soups, sauces and dips are on the shelves plus dried fruit and all the baking aids as well as condiments, spices and dried herbs. Local market ladies sell their own bottled concoctions of cooking sauces, usually excellent value and very tasty. Have fun experimenting.

In the refrigerated section you will find dairy products: cheeses of all sorts, butter, margarine plus lunch meats, bacon, sausage and delicatessen. Yogurt comes in every flavor imaginable, except natural. All food seems to be enhanced with honey or nuts or is toasted, roasted or heavily laced with high-fructose corn syrup, including savory foods.

Tea bags and coffee (ground and instant) are available in familiar brands. Try the local grown beans plus Colombian and Venezuelan coffees.

A selection of pulses, in colors you may not have seen before, plus dried beans of all sorts are available. Useful staples, but they require plenty of water for soaking and must be cooked correctly, preferably in a pressure cooker, for safe eating. If you like the small red lentils (delicious cooked half and half with rice) bring them with you as they are not available in the Caribbean. These lentils require no soaking nor particular cooking temperatures.

Fresh milk may be local or imported from the US. UHT milk is sold in plastic bottles or cartons; some cartons have a plastic snap pourer; to avoid splattering when opening the pourer, make a small slit with a sharp, pointed knife on the farther (up) side to allow air in. Dried milk is full cream and mixes easily with cold water. Nestlé is a familiar name, as well as the clas-

sic Klim that senior cruisers might remember from back then. Coffee whiteners are available as well as evaporated and condensed milk in cans.

Drinks

Rum is the traditional drink of choice in the Caribbean. The potent distillation of sugar cane residues, rum was developed during the sugar trade but is now mainly produced in Barbados and Trinidad. With a proof rating from 80 to 150 it is usually drunk with water, mixers or fruit juice as a punch. A Caribbean Rum Punch has a justifiable reputation, rambunctious as a pirate chief. Recipes vary widely and a rum punch may have the kick of a mule or the slow hand of a lover. Few sunsets are complete without a rum in your hand and someone to nudge.

Caribbean beer brands, lighter than English beer and always served cold, as well as German and American beers are available. Wine can be found in some supermarkets but the best buys are in the French Islands. One of the cheapest places to buy alcohol is in the duty free shops in Charlotte Amalie,

USVI, and the Cash & Carry in Road Town, Tortola, BVI. Prices get cheaper down island but Mount Gay is the connoisseur's choice.

Sodas in leading brands are here; you can also buy tonic water, Schweppes and own-brand, club soda and other carbonated drinks. Fruit juices, orange, grapefruit and many others are in the cool section. Coconut water, bottled, is a delightful refresher. Road side stall holders will, with the adroit flourish of a machete, decapitate a fresh nut for you to drink with a straw. Some nuts have a sweet jelly within, to be spooned out with a flake from the shell. Beware of coconut juice as it stains indelibly.

Galley items

Most of the items you might want in a kitchen or galley are readily available throughout the islands, bigger islands equal better selection. Here is a list of some of the more obvious items, all to be had in one store or another.

You will find paper towels, bathroom tissues, Kleenex and napkins as well as plates; some local, some imported brands. Paper plates are best supported (4–5 at a time) on woven rattan plates that hold the standard size. Peel off as used. Plastic disposable plates can be bought here too.

All the cleaning materials you could want are here, plus the things to apply them: brushes, sponges, abrasive pads, rubber gloves, brooms and dustpans. Vinegar, sold in gallon jugs, has many uses apart from salad. It will clean fresh epoxy off hands and remove salt stains from glass and plastic ports.

You can buy pots and pans (from the cheapest to high quality imported items), kettles, toasters, stainless cutlery, plus other kitchen equipment. I cannot think of any item I've needed in the galley that I haven't been able to find somewhere. The larger stores in major towns have all the electrical gadgets you could want–if you can power them. French islands sell 220v appliances and US Virgins work on 120v. Check each island before connecting to shore power.

14

The cruising life

Island Time

"Runnin' on Islan' Time" is the mantra for the Caribbean. The heat precludes running anywhere here, unless to the bar to catch the last drink of Happy Hour. Shop assistants will seem to dawdle off to fetch what you want but that's how everyone moves. If a mechanic tells you "tomorrow" it may turn out to be next week. Even LIAT, the local 20-seat airline, is affectionately known as Leave Island Any Time or Luggage In Another Terminal. To someone raised in temperatures seldom below 80°F your urgent need is just another job; it will all get done in the end. Huffing and puffing won't improve anyone's temper, and could show you up as yet another pushy foreigner. Adjust to Island Time and schedule enough of it into your plans to allow for drift.

What most cruisers have much of is time. To the cruiser there's time to "lime" (hang out with your friends), to go ashore and explore, or to just watch the sun set over another perfect scene. That is apart from the time to do all the routine jobs of stores and chores, not to mention those maintenance jobs. You'll find the day get so full that you'll wonder how you ever held a day job.

Cruising is all about making short passages and stopping frequently to explore and socialize. Try not to set deadlines for yourself and others.

Sightseeing

Each island has its own distinct culture and topography. Islands with high mountains are lusher and greener than their flatter neighbors, attracting more rain and allowing a wide agriculture. Tourism is the biggest earner but some islands, such as Dominica, that have no sandy beaches, are very poor,

Sugar production, part of island economy since the 17th century, is now on the decline. Many sugar mills like this one are all that's left of the old industry.

but charming in their simplicity. Other islands have sophisticated resorts and are more prosperous. Being proud of its heritage, each island has plenty to offer the visitor. The cruising guides give descriptive details of each island so you can plan to get the best out of your visit.

Transportation

Local public transportation is by maxi-taxis. These are 15-seater vans that ply the roads on designated routes on each island. There's seldom any timetable for the buses run frequently on the most popular routes and though there are fixed stops you can flag the maxi anywhere along the route; they don't like to miss a fare. Prices vary but are usually around $US1, depending on distance. The vehicles can be quite decrepit and the driving could be described as "enthusiastic" but the atmosphere is jolly and it's customary to say hello or at least smile and nod to everyone, when entering.

Special trips can usually be arranged with a private taxi. Share expenses by making a group. A taxi driver's local knowledge is usually very good, language is seldom a problem as English is spoken in most of the islands though you may have to listen carefully until you become accustomed to the accent. St. Vincent taxi drivers

Photo opposite: Public transport, island style, though this one is more for tourists. Most are the 14 seater minibus type; it's a friendly squash if you have children and shopping.

take the art to a new height and seem able to accomplish any task for the cruising sailor, no matter how bizarre and are a fund of information. English-speaking taxi drivers in the French islands aren't so common and their descriptions and explanations may be limited. French-speaking islanders seem disinclined to speak or understand anything but French, so brush up on your French.

In Trinidad, if you wish to go off the maxi routes in the capital, Port-of-Spain, you can hail any passing car with a registration plate marked 'H' as it is a taxi. These H cars also run prescribed routes, cost only 1 or 2 TT dollars and will stop anywhere they are hailed if they have a vacant seat. If they pass you by, don't worry, there'll be another one along in a minute.

Car rental is available in almost all the islands though the vehicle may have seen better days. Apart from the rental charge there will be insurance plus mileage. Rental cars may be earmarked by the local low life so leave nothing in it you can't afford to lose, even if it's locked in the trunk.

Bicycles are a useful addition to the cruising boat though I once stated publicly to the contrary and had to eat my words later. They are particularly useful when the boat is on the hard and there is a lot of traveling between yards, suppliers and shops. Good folding bikes need to be guarded, and not just from salt water, as they are currency. For some boats the only stowage is lashed on deck and whenever the bike is left aboard or ashore it should be protected with a very stout security device. There are several popular models, some with versions in stainless steel.

Eating out

This is usually cheap though some French islands can rival the mainland prices. Food is plentiful in the Caribbean, the climate brings an abundance of well-priced fruits and vegetables; imported items are more expensive, particularly apples.

Local cuisine is a terrific mix of the various cultures that have influenced the history of each island and the same dish will differ slightly from island to island, even from end to end of the same island. This makes enjoyable research. Hygiene standards are generally good and we've seldom heard of more than the occasional upset stomach. Hot chili sauce is a ubiquitous ingredient so you may want to order your food without.

Roti and other local dishes

One of the most popular meals to be found almost anywhere you go in the Caribbean, though more so in the Windwards, is the roti. Pronounced to rhyme with "boaty," it is one of the tastiest, cheapest and most easily obtained meals "to go." The roti is basically a chicken curry with vegetables, wrapped in a parcel of soft, spiced, dry pancake made of unleavened wholemeal flour, similar to an Indian chapati or Mexican flour tortilla. The filling can also be beef, pork, shrimp or just vegetables. Again, recipes vary from place to place, try them all to find your favorite.

Another popular snack-to-go is "doubles." These are palm-sized corn pancakes filled with chickpea mash and pickles, usually sold from a roadside stall or even Stop-me-and-buy-one man on a bicycle. The whole lot is expertly captured in a twist of greaseproof paper and away you go.

Other favorite foods are corn soup, thickened with lentils with slices of sweet corn and potato; cow heel soup with dumplings. Callaloo is a thick dark green soup made from the spinach-like dasheen leaf. Jonny cakes are palm-size flat rounds of deep fried bread dough. Sometimes called bakes, they are delicious alone or as a base for fish, mostly shark, or chicken. Goat meat is prepared mostly in casseroles. The meat of the conch can be tough but well beaten, mixed with herbs and spices, it makes tasty fritters or chowder. Coocoo is a solid yellow corn meal pudding with chopped vegetables served in slices; an excellent filler with callaloo. As one delightful stall holder remarked when she shared the recipe with me, "It fill yo' belly good." It certainly does.

Small, reasonably priced eateries can be found just about anywhere you go. Some of the more humble establishments might not appeal but you're sure to find somewhere that suits. The food is good, prices are right and the service is friendly.

Clubs

Belonging to a yacht club in the US sometimes has certain advantages when visiting other places. Being a member of one of the cruising clubs such as the Ocean Cruising Club (OCC) and the Seven Seas Cruising Association (SSCA) can bring you into contact with other cruising members when you run up your burgee in an anchorage. Both the above clubs issue periodical magazines with members' contributions about their travels and experiences, good and bad, that are an excellent source of information. The OCC has port officers around the globe who welcome contact for help and advice in their area; parties and Club meets are held worldwide throughout the year. Entry to the SSCA is via a proposal from a current member. The OCC requirement is for a 1000nm offshore passage. Your Caribbean 1500 passage will fit the bill nicely.

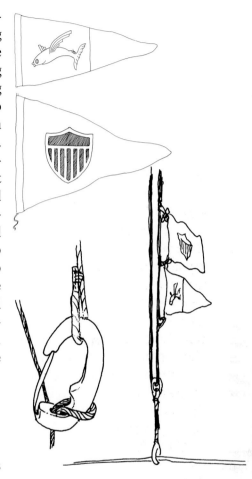

What's on?

Many of the popular long-stay anchorages have a calendar of regular events such as weekly barbecues, pot luck dinners or even, as in Trinidad, film nights. Asking around the anchorage on arrival will usually elicit the diary of What's on. There may be a daily net on VHF giving details of weather, local news and social events.

A quick fix for flag and burgee deployment to span differing flag sizes. Plastic hooks are easily adjusted on an 'endless' halyard, tensioned with bungy cord.

Some places publish a booklet listing all the information the cruiser needs. In Trinidad the *Boater's Directory* is an invaluable source of local information, distributed free at marinas and boat yards. Free monthly papers such as *Compass, All At Sea* and *Island's Nautical Scene* are distributed widely throughout the Caribbean.

Pot luck

These suppers are a very popular pastime with cruisers. Sometimes they are a regular event in an established location such as a yacht club or marina. Here you might find a fixed barbecue, tables and chairs and the strong possibility of a bar. Otherwise, pot luck dinners tend to be spontaneous or, if regular, less formal than at a club. Popular anchorages usually have them regularly during the season, held on the beach or a handy open space.

For these events it is customary for everyone to bring a large dish of starters, entrée or dessert to a central location and everyone helps themselves. You provide your own plates, cutlery and drinks. The occasion is frequently lively and is an excellent way to meet your fellow cruisers.

Pot luck is also a good way of entertaining aboard with two or three couples gathered on one boat, all contributing something to the meal. This way there is no obligation to "owe hospitality" as at home. Not that cruisers keep tabs, for you will find that favors are passed on rather than returned and what goes around, comes around.

Movies

Films are very popular and you will find a movie theater in most of the large islands. While the building, décor and furniture might be a little run down, prices are reasonable and security is good. You might not, however, consider dark enclosed places desirable with regard to catching colds, etc. Some marinas have regular film showings on video. Some of the larger islands have video rental shops.

Carnival

The annual carnival in each island is big business and preparations start almost the day after the last one finishes. The traditional time for carnival is linked to Easter. Shrove Tuesday, which falls 40 days before Easter Day, is the last day before the Lenten fast and islands hold a one- or two-day carnival that ends on the Tuesday.

Trinidad has the largest carnival, celebrating with daily events for the four weeks leading up to Shrove Tuesday, with the last two days being the frenzied culmination of all the parades, the largest floats and the final competitions to decide the winners of the various categories.

Other islands hold their carnivals at different times so as not to clash and allow people to enjoy several celebrations during the year. Most islands have tourist offices where you can find such information as well as other useful material, maps and guides, etc. Inquiring around the anchorage will also give you an idea of what's going on at any particular time.

Children play a special part in Carnival and are captivating with their uninhibited performances on stage.

Museums

Even the tiniest island usually has at least one museum. The islanders are very proud of their individual history and make great efforts to preserve houses, artefacts and customs. Slavery and the subsequent liberation are well documented and although the subject is seldom brought up openly it remains a quiet undercurrent and the prudent cruiser will respect the feelings of present day descendants. Many islands have restored old plantation houses as hotels and restaurants. St. Martin has the only butterfly farm in the Caribbean.

Swimming and snorkeling

Enjoying the sea is a large part of the fun of being in the Caribbean. With warm clear water over coral, the sea life is colorful and abundant so that diving off the boat for a cooling splash or donning mask and snorkel for an in-depth look becomes a daily event. Even non-swimmers can enjoy snorkeling once they gain the confidence to put their faces in the water. The human body naturally floats face down and will not start to sink until the head is raised; in fact it is quite difficult to keep your legs and face down at the same time. Start off standing in waist-deep water with properly adjusted mask and snorkel and get used to breathing with head immersed and you'll be floating in no time.

Swimming hazards

The hazards are few and all easily avoidable.

- **Sunburn** Wearing an old T-shirt while snorkeling helps to protect the back from sunburn though neck and backs of legs may get caught, use sunblock for these skin areas.
- **Drifting** Just gazing and paddling along in the warm water, it's easy to lose track of time and place. While tides are negligible there are currents, stronger in some places than others. Be aware of which way the current might be going and swim up current to drift down or look up frequently to take bearings remembering it will take you longer to swim back up current to regain your boat.
- **Other traffic** A snorkeler is not very obvious to a speeding dinghy or other craft. The buzz of an outboard is audible underwater and on hearing it the swimmer should check to locate the boat and its intentions. Some snorkelers attach themselves to a bright float to alert other craft but in the end it's up to the swimmer to be vigilant.
- **Fire coral and other stingers** Fire coral is bright red and burns the skin it touches. Only set foot (or hand) on sand or clear rock as the delicate surface of all corals is destroyed by touch. Skin grazes from any coral can become infected quickly.
- **Sea urchins** sit on the rocks waiting for the unwary foot. The spines snap off under the skin and break up when probed. Painful at first, the wound gradually suppurates after a few days and the spines are exuded with the pus. Some people reckon that vinegar or lime juice applied immediately helps to dissolve the spines but medical advice should be sought.
- **Sting rays** sting when stepped on or threatened. As they tend to bury themselves in the sand with only the eyes showing they are difficult to spot but don't often settle in standing depth. A prospective flap with your flipper to disturb the sand will startle a resting ray and give him a chance to escape. They're not really interested in you but can attack if they think you're getting too close for comfort. The huge spotted eagle rays are no threat but a wonder to watch.
- **Sharks** There are sharks in the Caribbean but you'll seldom see them as they tend to keep to deep water. They may sometimes be attracted by spear fishing, or blood in the water, yours or the fish you just speared. Spear fishing is forbidden in some islands. Check with Customs.
- **Barracuda** will hang motionless and watch you while you snorkel; just nod politely and move on quietly. Moray eels sit poking their heads out of rocky holes so don't poke yours in.
- **Most wild life** is only too happy to go about its business quietly ignoring you if you pose no threat to them; it's a case of "do-as-you-would-be-done-by."

Scuba diving

Diving is popular and many cruisers carry their own tanks and compressors but there are dive centers on many islands where you will find qualified instructors and gear to rent at reasonable prices and where your tanks can be tested and refilled.

For a lot of reasons renting gear makes sense, especially for a diver new to Caribbean diving. It is also better to get a certificate in the Caribbean where all instruction, plus your test dive, is done in clear warm and open water rather than in a more northern place where you'll learn in a swimming pool and test dive in cold murky waters. PADI and NAUI are equally good certifications but if you are short of time or not sure it's for you then the Resort Course will have you doing a simple dive after only a morning's instruction. Scuba gear takes up a lot of space and needs fanatical maintenance to remain safe; renting can be cheaper and easier unless you are a truly dedicated diver.

If the sport grabs you, you can go for further instruction, extended dives and full certification. Diving with local instructors will give you the benefit of getting to the best dive sights in their fast boats. They will know the hang outs of the most spectacular fish and coral and can guide you through a drift dive where you get swept along by the current in the company of huge rays while gawking at the passing show.

The International Code flag 'A' for 'I have a diver down' is not seen so often in the Caribbean as the US dive flag which has a red background with a white diagonal line, not to be confused with the national flag of Trinidad which is similar. If you choose not to dive with a dive center, always dive with a buddy and display a dive flag. Some islands restrict you to diving with their centers; don't ignore this rule.

Fishing

Fishing for a free dinner sounds like fun but in some islands, the British Virgin Islands and St. Lucia for example, a fishing permit is required and spear fishing is forbidden in other islands also. Reef fish can cause ciguatera poisoning (see Chapter 17) but deep water fish are safe. Check with Customs on clearing into a country for their regulations on fishing. Local fishermen can get upset if they see their livelihood threatened. Between the islands, trolling a line will usually produce something for the pan but you'll need to be quick reeling in or a bigger fish will take your supper. There are fishing tackle shops in some islands; Wallace & Co Fishing Supplies in Bequia are very helpful with advice on the season's favorite lure. A cleaning and gutting board rigged on the stern rail is a handy aid.

This good-sized dorado will make excellent eating – a welcome addition to the menu.

Barbecues

Barbecues are a good way of cooking meat and fish, keeping the smell and heat out of the galley. Cruising boats can usually be spotted by the barbecue on the stern rail. Some go for charcoal which you can get in the larger islands. Propane, either in standard tanks or in a screw-on minitank, is the other option. Propane has the advantage of being cleaner with no residue to dispose of but the die-hards swear that charcoals gives a better taste; you take your choice.

On-board entertainment

Installing a 12-V quality car hi-fi system will enable you to listen to radio, audio tapes and CDs. Personal stereos are fun to have to while away a night watch or dull maintenance job. All magnetic tape/film deteriorates more quickly in the heat and humidity. CDs fare better. Fitting quality speakers linked to your hi-fi in the saloon will reward you with almost concert standards and you can wind up the volume without disturbing the anchorage. If fitting cockpit speakers, remember that sound carries over water and your particular brand of recorded audio performance may not go down so well with others.

TV is alive and well in the islands but you will need a TV receiver suitable to the local transmission system which, in the Caribbean, is NTSC, except in the French islands where the Secam system is used. If you plan to watch local TV, home videos from your camcorder, videos you bring with you, or might acquire or rent along the way, you will need a multi-standard TV-VCR that includes NTSC, as well as Secam/PAL. Probably your best bet for choice and price will be in Philipsburg, Great Bay on Sint Maarten (the Dutch side of St. Martin). This is a Duty Free port and you will find multi-standard TV-VCRs readily available plus a wide range of other electronic equipment. While the purists scorn TV, many yachts now sport TVs of all sizes. All large islands broadcast a creditable TV service with up-to-date news and weather. While you might not care about the state of the local politics or banana crop, local weather will be your concern. Hurricane watching, particularly at the end and beginning of the season is advisable. Even during the sailing season high and low pressure systems form and pass over the area and need to be taken into account when passage planning (see Chapter 11). With a TV-VCR you'll also be able to watch and swap videos. So you think you won't miss TV? Wait and see; it gets dark at 1800. Check to see how many boats sport the tell-tale disc-like multi-directional TV antenna or the flickering blue glow through a port.

Beware of siting a TV antenna close to any other active antenna, i.e., one supplied with 12-V power to make it more effective. An active GPS antenna could cause interference on some TV channels. If you have poor reception on any particular channel try switching off the active antenna.

Books, videos and swaps
Cruisers are avid readers but books are expensive and choice limited in the islands so you will find book and video swaps wherever cruisers hang out: cafes, boat yards and Laundromats.

Cameras, camcorders and film

It would seem almost a crime not to record your time in the Caribbean, given the many easy ways of doing so. Cameras, camcorders, video cassettes, discs and film however, are all susceptible to the heat and salt atmosphere of the tropics. Guard all sensitive equipment from direct sun and salt spray. Keeping cameras and lenses in a sealed container with bags of silica gel helps to delay the onset of micro bacterial growth.

Keep fresh film refrigerated in a dedicated sealed box before and after exposure. Don't leave film in the camera too long. All popular brands of color negative film are available throughout the islands. To ensure the freshest stock, buying from an air-conditioned shop with high turnover is usually better than the corner emporium with doors open to the hot dusty street. There are 1-hour labs in the towns and tourist centers for color film but few

Boat cards

Most cruisers carry boat cards to give to new friends, giving the boat's name and perhaps her silhouette, names of skipper and wife, plus other details such as mailing address and phone number, e-mail and website address, Ham call sign, etc. It's the easiest way to keep a record of cruising friends. If you have a computer and printer aboard you can make your own cheap and unique card with a picture of your own boat, changing the details as and when necessary.

labs that can handle slide processing. Bring a supply of your favorite slide film.

We have found our digital camera increasingly useful. With the digital pictures downloaded onto the laptop and some text added, then printed out in color, letters home give a vivid impression of your cruising life. Being able to erase unwanted pictures has saved a fortune on film and processing; yet we can bore folk rigid with "another day in paradise." Attaching digital pictures to e-mail is fun also.

Video film makes a wonderful record of your travels; remember to take the camcorder ashore to record more than just "views from the boat" which tend to be repetitive after a while.

Be cautious when pointing your camera at local people. Some people object strongly, which is their right, and if you want to record some local color it is only polite to ask first if there is any objection. You can throw in some sweetener such as "I want to show your lovely island to my family back home," which will be no lie. School teachers are particularly respected and one cruiser always made it plain that "my students will learn so much about life in St. Lucia" or wherever she happened to be. The French islanders seem more sensitive than others. Some subjects might ask for a fee, the decision is yours.

Pets

Many boats have pets aboard, mostly cats, but you will also see dogs, canaries, parrots or parakeets, and even more exotic creatures kept captive as pets.

Cats
Cats adapt particularly well to life afloat, especially if introduced to it when young. Being solitary by nature, they do not mind being left all day while

Nearly every island boasts its share of the best beaches – or prettiest, longest, widest, pinkest, whitest, most bars, quietest etc. One island boasts a different beach for every day of the year (and we can verify Martinique's claim of a black volcanic sand beach right next to a pure white one).

Caribbean sunsets; there are never two alike. After the heat of the day, sitting quietly in the cockpit with your favorite drink, perhaps swapping yarns with friends from another boat, is not a bad way to end the day.

Many islands have mountainous rain forests with waterfalls, and it's worth the climb for the reward of a cooling plunge in a rock pool, before descending to the heat of the lowlands again.

Subsistence fishing might be all that some islanders manage. In this quiet bay we watched a group of fishermen haul in these long nets, catching only a handful of small fish that they share out with friends and family.

Flowers seem to try to outdo each other with color and mass. Bougainvillaea, plumbago and oleander grow like weeds, and trees such as the flamboyia live up to their name with clouds of scarlet blossom.

The Tobago Cays is a popular anchorage with three tiny uninhabited islets. The calm crystal waters are protected by a horseshoe reef and boats lie steady to the constant breeze. It's quite a concept to realize that, looking east beyond the curl of the surf, there is nothing between you and Africa. There are no facilities so be fully provisioned if you want to stay a few days.

The Museum at Nelson's Dockyard, Antigua. This classically beautiful building, over 200 years old, once housed Nelson's officers. The whole dockyard is well preserved and the many buildings offer an interesting glimpse of life in the old man's time.

The narrow sand spit at the northern end of Mayreau, in the Grenadines, guards Saltwhistle Bay from the trade winds and provides a calm anchorage. Ashore there is a small restaurant set back under the trees.

Carnival plays an important part in island life and though traditionally timed to end before Lent, many islands now stagger their dates through the year so as not to clash. You can progress from one carnival to another, if you have the stamina.

This clapboard (pronounced clabberd) house is an all-wood structure and typical of the 'newer' Caribbean architecture, being only about 100 years old. The wood, often painted with pastel colors, was usually imported.

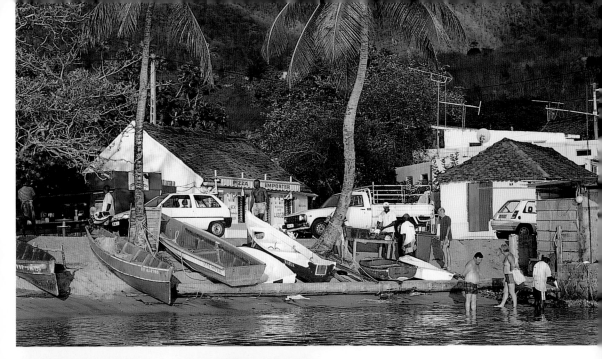

Fishermen's dinghies pulled up on the beach at Anse de Chaudierre, Petit Anse d'Arlet, Martinique. Usually made on the island, these heavy open boats, decorated in bright colors, are powered by hefty outboards and can be seen with nets and gear far out to sea.

This charming 'gingerbread' house is a boutique for the well-to-do residents on the exclusive island of Mustique, who have included Mick Jagger, David Bowie and the late Princess Margaret. Even for the less affluent cruiser, a day visit is worth it to walk through the grounds of The Old Cotton House, or sip a sundowner at Basil's Bar on the beach.

Colorful market stalls along the waterfront in Marigot, St. Martin. Carvings in wood, shell and stone show the islanders' talents, while fruits and vegetables thought exotic at home are everyday fare.

Masquerading (dressing up in fantastic costumes) is what Carnival is all about. Designers start on next year's patterns shortly after the end of the previous year. The costumes for the star performers can be huge, and the man or woman parading must be pretty fit to dance throughout the whole day.

Feeding the fish takes on a whole new meaning at Norman Island, BVIs, when you snorkel with a fist full of bread. Small fishy noses will push fearlessly at your hand and will follow you around in clouds. Snorkelling is one of the delights of cruising in the Caribbean and is a skill easily mastered by even the most timid swimmer.

Home delivery, madam? No problem. If you can't get to the market, the market will come to you in Rodney Bay, St. Lucia. This enterprising trader has decorated his dory with palm fronds and a roof to shade the fruit and vegetables, though it's a miracle it doesn't turn turtle.

One of the street markets in Fort de France, Martinique. The familiar bustle and enticing smells are what make these markets so entertaining. Business is brisk and the French islands seem more cosmopolitan than their laid-back neighbors.

An archetypal beach: irresistible crystal turquoise water lapping the white sand beach shaded by frondy palms – the stuff dreams are made of.

Night falls quickly in the tropics and the hours of daylight vary little throughout the year. Getting anchored by tea time guarantees a ringside seat to spot the rare green flash that sometimes shows as the sun sinks below the horizon. Being mostly away from the loom of bright lights the stars have a mass and intensity not seen in cities.

Wide sweeping bays backed by tree-clad hills are typical of island anchorages, but careful scrutiny of the chart may reveal hidden coral reefs or sand banks. Ask yourself why that nice clear space has no boats and the answer may well be some hazard just under the water waiting to trap the unwary.

the crew go ashore and are content to find a cool place to nap. Their toilet requirements are straightforward with a litter box; cat litter is available in most supermarkets as well as a range of pet foods and other requirements. Cats swim well but seldom choose to do so; a plaited rope secured to the side or stern reaching to water level will soon teach Ginger to climb back up after a miscalculation. Rinse his fur with fresh water or he'll lick the salt which is not good for him. Cats, while being great companions, don't do too well as boat guardians.

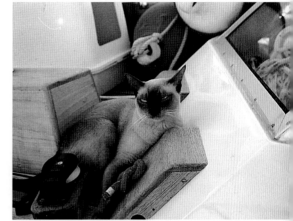

Dogs

Dogs, on the other hand, being territorial, make good boat guards but if you are thinking about bringing a dog with you, or acquiring one once you are in the Caribbean, there are some issues that need careful consideration.

A dog by nature, even a small one, needs daily exercise. Some islands do not allow non-local animals ashore. St. Lucia is rabies-free and has zero tolerance for foreign animals, regardless of their health certificates. There is a deadly little heartworm parasite on most of the islands that can infect your pet. Most islands have qualified veterinary surgeons but if your pet is sick on an island where it is forbidden ashore, you will be faced with the cost of the vet's visit aboard. Dogs need a lot more water in the tropics; you'll need to add that to your daily requirements.

A dog's toilet is not so easy to manage as a cat's. Taking Fido ashore twice a day for exercise and finding an appropriate spot for him to foul, without leaving a mess for others to walk in or pick up after him, could take a lot of time out of your day. Some cruisers allow the dog to foul on the foredeck, sometimes on a special mat. The mat is then washed off with sea water periodically. Man's best friend is a pack animal and will follow his leader anywhere but many howl their objections when Man goes ashore without him. Think about whether these restrictions are acceptable to your dog and yourself.

Should you want to take a trip home or inland, or even just to stay away overnight, Fido will have to be cared for.

Etiquette

How to deal with Customs Officers is a complete subject in itself and is discussed in Chapter 15. For the rest, observation, common sense and good manners are your best guide to getting the greatest enjoyment out of your visit.

What not to be overheard saying

Although initially it might seem you've arrived in paradise, all the Caribbean islands are poor by U.S. standards. The longer you stay, the more you become aware of the sometimes desperate differences between "us and them." Even the humblest, most run-down boat could be worth more than some islanders earn in a lifetime, while the price of a well-found cruising boat may buy an entire village. Bearing this in mind, it is not a good idea to flash your wallet around or talk loudly in public about the amount of money you've just spent on your boat or "how *cheap* this place is."

That last remark, prefixed with a statement that the owner had just spent $5,000 on his boat, was uttered loudly while standing in a crowded bus queue of mixed company. It did not do a lot for public relations when one considers some in the queue, who were lucky enough to be employed, might earn less than $10 a day.

When ashore or talking in public try to use more flattering phrases and keep the word *cheap* for onboard talk.

Smile

The Caribbeans are a smiling people so relax and smile too when you talk. This is important to improve the image that foreigners get for appearing "superior." A smile, eye contact and saying "Please" and "Thank You" will go a long way toward promoting good will. Most people say "excuse me" when walking past you in the grocery store aisle even though there might be plenty of room and no one need move aside; they just say it anyway.

Dress and dress code

You will see that local people dress modestly, particularly the women. Religion plays a large part in island life. Most people are Christian, there are Hindu and Muslim minorities. The churches and temples are enthusiastically filled on holy days with the congregation dressed in its best. For everyday life, women dress modestly, dresses are mostly with sleeves and a skirt below the knee and no cleavage. The tourists are obvious in their short shorts, skimpy tops and plunging necklines.

It's sometimes tempting, especially if one has been working on the boat, to nip ashore or into town wearing your working T-shirt with a pair of cut-off shorts. But casual clothes are cheap in the islands, and soap and water is plentiful. Cruisers tend to get a bad press with islanders, sometimes justifiably, so it helps not to add fuel to the fire.

Going topless for women, even aboard your own boat, is not appropriate in sight of others, though you will see Europeans of both sexes who go naked in crowded anchorages. That might be acceptable in their homelands but is offensive in the Caribbean and brings ridicule or worse to cruisers generally. Certain resorts are more permissive. In a deserted anchorage you can do what you like.

Dressing for the occasion

Most cruisers' wardrobes are restricted by the size of their clothing lockers. Cruising in the tropics doesn't necessarily mean fewer clothes and the picture of the tropical cruiser dressed only in cut-off shorts and a baseball cap is not quite complete. The heat demands frequent changes of clothes from casual to smart casual. It's worth packing a sweatshirt and sweatpants, for night passages, even in the tropics, can be surprisingly cool with the down draft from the mainsail. You need clothing for all sailing conditions.

As mentioned earlier, island women dress modestly; do likewise if you don't want to attract undesirable attention. Avoid skimpy clothes, cleavage revealing tops or short shorts when going ashore or into town. You will seldom see a Caribbean woman wearing shorts or a plunging neckline unless she is very young. It is really a matter of respecting the standards of a predominantly religious community.

You will find plenty of clothing stores in the tourist centers but, apart from T-shirts, the tourist boutiques tend to be a little expensive. Once away from the tourist routes you will find simple clothes at reasonable prices.

Underwear

Cotton is the best fiber for most underwear. Women should bring a good supply of bras and briefs as the tropical heat causes elastic to go into meltdown fairly quickly. The design of bras available in the islands may not suit your build; this isn't critical with briefs but choice is limited. Hand laundry, the washing machines plus the sun soon leave clothes looking a little tired and gray.

Day wear

The ubiquitous T-shirt is probably the key item in the cruising wardrobe. T-shirts are a mainstay of the Caribbean tourist market and you will find stalls everywhere selling T-shirts in a dazzling array of designs. The thinner weight makes them cooler plus easier to wash and dry. Wear them until they start to look less than pristine, then demote them to boat work shirts and rags and buy more. T-shirts are cheap and it helps the local economy.

Buttoned shirts in woven cotton make good going-ashore wear, (the collar on tailored shirts can be turned up to protect the neck from sunburn) and worn with shorts or a skirt of a reasonable length, they make a better impression than a wilting T-shirt.

Shorts of decent length are the basic apparel for both sexes. Lightweight trousers and lightweight longer skirts are useful also as they are cooler than denim as well as protecting the skin. We have found the range of sunscreening fabric used in the better quality outdoor clothing brands to be excellent for comfort and protection as well as looking smart without being formal. The fabric has a pleasant feel and is specially woven from a synthetic fiber that wicks perspiration away from the skin, keeping the wearer cool and comfortable. The garments are well designed for ease of movement with plenty of vents, numerous pockets; they also wash easily and dry quickly. Though costing more than ordinary clothes this type of clothing will repay the initial expense many times over in looks, longevity and comfort.

The pareo or sarong is an easy garment, nothing more than a large rectangle of very light weight cotton fabric that can be worn in innumerable ways to flatter every figure. You can buy pareos just about everywhere in the Caribbean in bright colors or make your own; they are light, practical and pack flat—excellent for taking home as presents. They are great around the boat and the beach but not for going ashore or into town.

Making your own clothes

If you have a sewing machine, making clothes is easy for fabrics are cheap in the islands, especially Trinidad which is a sewer's paradise. Bring your favorite basic paper patterns as they are expensive and the range limited. Sewing accessories are plentiful in Trinidad but less so in the islands. All notions are available but not terribly good.

Trinidad is the island of Carnival and seamstresses will run up any garment or bed linen for a very reasonable price; they will also copy a favorite garment faithfully.

The range of fabrics in Trinidad is huge, running from the flimsiest chiffons, through cottons to fantasy fabrics. Upholstery fabrics as well as Sunbrella, Texaline and other yacht canvas are available making Trinidad a mecca for boat refurbishing.

Outer gear

Adequate foul weather gear will probably be on your list if you are coming from the north, though you won't need it too often in the island chain. A lightweight rain slicker of the sort that folds up into its own pocket with matching trousers, or a lightweight cotton mix jacket are useful when you come back late to the boat.

Footwear

The range of sports footwear available to the cruiser today is enormous but buying quality pays dividends for the better made footwear survives the rough treatment of shipboard life. Toes are very vulnerable to all the deck hardware that lies in wait. Cracked and broken toes are painful and most accidents can be prevented by wearing shoes on deck. Good leather deck shoes, preferably lace-up, give better traction than bare feet and, in the tropics where the deck can be uncomfortably hot, protect feet from being burnt. Feet sometimes have to double as extra hands and you might need to hold down a line, chain or piece of equipment. Obviously, care should be taken that there's no risk of line/chain snagging around the foot and causing injury. Trainers with non-marking soles are popular footwear though they can make your feet hot.

Going ashore barefoot in the mistaken image of a latter day Robinson Crusoe is a mistake. Docks and pontoons have splinters or nails sticking up and even the smallest lesion will quickly fester in the heat. Boat yards will have all sorts of debris just waiting for a tender foot. Pavements and roads will be dirty, dusty and oily, while grass and scrub may harbor ticks, parasites and other biters. The type of open sandals with tough sculptured soles and Velcro straps make excellent cruiser footwear. Robust and light, they give good traction in and out of water and provide cool and strong protection for cruising feet ashore or aboard. You may need to jump out of the dinghy into shallow water, knowing that your feet are protected from injury on rocks, pebbles, sand or coral while not losing your shoes to the undertow. Rock hoppers are an up-market beach shoe, found in dive shops. With a thick rubber sole and upper made from open-work nylon

Above: Tough open sandals with Velcro straps. Below: Lightweight Rock-hopper shoes, ideal for wading in the shallows.

or wetsuit fabric, these shoes totally enclose the feet but shed water quickly, protecting from injury though possibly not from sea urchin spines.

Flip flops can be lethal on board but are useful for that trip to the toilet/ shower block ashore where they will help prevent foot infections. Leather shoes and sandals are more comfortable than plastic in the heat.

Sailing boots are useful to protect feet when cleaning barnacles off the anchor chain or washing down the deck.

Headgear

Shade for the head is essential in the tropics but there is more to headgear than the ubiquitous baseball cap though it is a very useful item. Caps provide no protection for tender ear tops and napes. A canvas hat with all round brim and retaining straps is better and easy to fold and stuff into a pocket or a bag. Tilly hats with their strap preventers provide good protection, are washable and almost bullet-proof. They also float long enough for you to retrieve them if they should take a dip in the water.

There are hats that have a peak with fold-down sides and back brim which pop-stud out of the way when not wanted. The naval look gives you a certain air of authority, warranted or not. Ashore, wide brimmed straw hats are comfortable and you can have fun discovering that, in the tropics at midday, you can stand in the shade of your own hat. You will also find local made palm frond hats woven while you watch. These start out bright green before drying to a pale beige. They last surprisingly well but don't get overcharged for them.

Slow your pace

The pace of life is slower in the Caribbean. We in the US and in Europe are used to living in the fast lane, getting everything done at breakneck speed, instant everything. It can be difficult to understand the more laid back attitude in the tropics. New cruisers need to adjust to the different mindset, attitudes and behavior in the tropics. After generations of growing up in temperatures seldom less than 80° people move at a gentle pace to conserve energy. Be kind to yourself also, the heat can be very enervating and if you try to maintain your regular pace, your body may rebel. Observe the local greeting, "Takin' it easy, mon," and adjust to Island Time.

Boat boys

Local "boys" will vie with each other to be of service to you in any way they can. They'll offer to wash your boat, take a line ashore, take your garbage, sell you produce, artefacts and much else besides. They can be pushy.

Accept the help you want but don't be harrassed into any business you don't want. Never get into an argument but trying to say "No," politely all the time is a strain. We have found the phrase "Not today, thank you," a courteous way of avoiding conflict. Be sure to agree to terms before any business begins and confirm which type of dollar you both mean, US or EC. If you are at all unsure or unhappy with the arrangement, smile politely, say you've changed your mind and go below or push off to another anchorage.

Never buy coral goods from locals. It is illegal to take coral and they may tell all sorts of fancy stories about how it's not really coral, or it's a certain sort that is permitted. Not true; don't buy it and don't give them your garbage to take ashore. See below.

Waste disposal

In the Caribbean the problem is becoming greater each year as more tourists–including cruising boats–come to enjoy the benefits of island life.

Don't leave garbage, no matter how well sealed, anywhere where animals and children can ransack it. In some of the poorer islands, local boys will offer to take your garbage ashore. This may seem like a kind offer but very often the courier will forage through your waste, no matter how stinking, take what he can use and leave the rest to its fate wherever.

The subject of holding tanks for gray and black water is discussed in Chapter 5.

Social life

Socializing is a delight for most cruisers but remember that noise carries well over water. In a crowded anchorage, a boisterous cockpit crowd in their cups after midnight aboard the *Jolly Joker* will hardly be popular with those not part of the throng. Having said that, you may find, as most cruisers do, that late nights will become a thing of the past. The tendency is to retire early and rise early but no less fun is had for all that.

Running the engine or noisy generator after sundown is something "gentlemen don't do" though sometimes it is unavoidable. In some lonesome cove you can do what you like.

A family Christmas dinner at The Gingerbread House, Bequia followed later by a starlit stroll along the beach.

Live-aboards

The term "live-aboards" is sometimes used for cruisers who spend more than just the annual holidays on their boats. To outsiders the term tends to suggest those somewhat ragged, in the state of ship and crew. You will see some pretty unappetizing boats, crews and flags; fortunately they are in the minority but, as usual, they are the ones by whom the rest of us are judged by the locals. Aim to project your best image. The axiom Leave a Clean Wake may sound old-fashioned but it helps to leave a good impression and foster improved relations with our host countries.

15

Formalities & finance

Customs and Immigration

It is the responsibility of the master of every vessel to contact the Customs Office immediately upon arrival in a foreign port. Arrangements must then be made for an officer to visit the ship or for the master to go to the Custom's Office with ship's papers, a crew list, passports of all crew on board (alive or dead) plus the clearance papers from his last port of call.

In the Caribbean you will be visiting the Customs office at the port of entry for each new island territory to request free pratique. Your yellow "Q" flag plus correct courtesy flag should be flying from the appropriate spreaders before you enter territorial waters. Carry several copies of the crew list which includes ship's name, tonnage and home port plus all crew names, nationalities and passport numbers. Each child aboard should have his or her own passport (see Chapter 3).

The Captain will be required to fill in one or several forms and answer such questions that the Customs Officer might ask, i.e. the reason for visiting and the length of intended stay. The Captain may have to declare the amount of stores, liquor and other goods on board. (The word *drugs* is used for legal as well as illegal substances so it's as well to carry a list of all medications carried aboard, stating which are prescribed and that you carry only permitted drugs for your personal use; a doctor's letter confirming prescribed drugs for the crew helps. Narcotics, even if they are pain relievers such as codeine, are of interest to Customs. In 20 years we've never been questioned, but Customs may board your ship on a whim). When all is satisfactory you will be issued an entry permit.

Customs Officers come in all sizes and types and have to face a throng of assorted ill-prepared foreigners each day. It pays to be the soul of patience and propriety and present yourself in a businesslike fashion: buttoned shirt and clean slacks or shorts, carrying papers tidily in a water-resistant holder. French Customs officers are among the friendliest, best organized and least officious.

Immigration will require a crew list with the names of all persons on board (within our time Trinidad was demanding to know how many stowaways were onboard).

Crew joining ship and arriving by some other means (plane, cruise liner, other yacht, etc.) should carry a letter of authority from the Captain, stating the reasons for joining, length of stay and port of departure. Crew joining and leaving from the same place, with a valid return ticket home, should have little problem.

Customs Officers and offices differ from island to island. Some, as in the French islands, make life easy with a single page of questions in French and English; the whole business seldom takes more than 10 minutes. In other islands you can spend hours in a hot airless office, crowded in with other tired and irritable applicants, filling in pages of questions in triplicate and then have to repeat the whole process with the Immigration Office which might be on the other side of town. Sometimes the Port Officer must be visited also. Some islands have streamlined the procedure and, once legally admitted to an island or its group, you are not required to check in again until leaving.

Government House sits between the palm trees on Jost van Dyke. Just stroll up the beach to check in with Customs and Immigration then take in a cool beer at Foxy's Bar.

A close study of the latest cruising guide for the area is advisable to check on opening times for Customs and Immigration offices. Some offices are open 24 hours a day but if you come outside standard office hours (say 0900 to 1600) you might be charged an overtime rate. Arriving breathless at 1555 might not suffice as, by the time your papers have been processed, you will have run into overtime and a charge may be levied. In islands where the offices are open only during the day, report at the earliest opportunity. In countries such as Trinidad, where the offices are open 24 hours a day, you must report immediately on arrival, day or night. If you don't want to pay the overtime rates, time your arrival well within the non-overtime hours. Be aware that national holidays count as overtime and as some holidays are determined by celestial factors, the exact date isn't known until the last moment. Some islands may have Customs half-way up the west coast which means traipsing there before stopping anywhere else. Loitering in a quiet outer bay until opening time could land you a hefty fine if spotted.

The only safe way is to play strictly by the rules. Unfortunately, island goal posts have a habit of changing without notice and their rules can be open to interpretation by the Officer of the Day. Other cruisers are one of the best sources on the latest state of play, good or bad. Radio nets will usually bring forth relevant information on request.

Length of stay

When asked how long you wish to stay do not reply "How long may I stay?" This response, even said with the most innocent smile, will trigger the suspicion that you want to stay permanently. Check beforehand on the maximum time allowed for that island or country and ask for it, even if you intend to leave sooner. (If you intend to return, check if there is a minimum return time.) The maximum allowed does not guarantee the maximum granted. If you are only passing through and intend to stay for two days, ask for two weeks. The chances are that you may have reason to need the extra time because of parts failure—or a party—and asking for an extension is time consuming and not always given.

Foreign vessels are restricted by each island's regulations and it is as well to check with Customs and Immigration on current regulations. Each island or group has its own laws and as these are subject to change it is not possible to state the facts here with any certainty. For most cruising boats and crews, visits of up to a month are usually not a problem and with some islands, three months may be permitted. Longer visits will generally need to be well supported, such as hauling the boat for storage, work being done by a local boat yard or serious medical treatment.

Speeding up Customs and Immigration clearance

The following is some of the information that you may be required to give when entering a new country. Make sure that you have all this information to hand on arrival at Customs and Immigration. See further notes below.

- *Documents* Ship's registation document; crew list; passports for all crew with name, date and place of birth, nationality, passport number, date of issue, where issued, date of expiration; position on board; clearance from previous port, (usually this information is requested on the forms supplied).
- *Details* Arrival/departure date; arrival time; berth/anchorage where vessel is located; last port visited; next port to be visited; expected departure date or length of stay; activity (private/pleasure); port of registry of vessel; date of registry of vessel; year of construction; USCG boat documentation; gross tonnage; net tonnage (if available); type of vessel; number of masts; hull material; hull color; engine make; engine HP; overall length; beam; draft; radio call sign; flag or country ensign; EPIRB details including ID; liferaft details—make and number of persons; name of owner(s) of vessel.
- *Crew* In addition to the above you might be asked for the number of crew and/or passengers embarking or disembarking. Remember that passengers would normally be paying guests and unless you are operating a charter vessel you are unlikely to have passengers on board. Friends cruising with you will be crew. If you are the Captain, your spouse is most likely to be the First Mate, who is recognized, after the Captain or Master, as having authority.

Documents

The two most valuable documents are your passport and the ship's registration document.

Keeping ship's papers and passports in good condition is necessary on a boat, for the humid atmosphere can cause deterioration. Ziplocs are useful for preserving the valuable documents such as passports, ship's registration documents and other vital information that might suffer from the dampness. Keep each passport in its own sealable bag. Photocopies of documents are not accepted.

Passports

It is usual for the Captain to hold the passports of all crew aboard his ship and he is responsible for the actions of his crew when ashore or if involved with any nefarious activities. Each crew member should carry several copies of his passport photo as some ports may require a copy for their files.

Carrying a photocopy of your passport provides you with identification in countries where citizens carry official ID. A photocopy of each crew member's passport should be included in the panic bag. Immigration takes a dim view of the bedraggled survivor crawling up the beach claiming to be a United States citizen if he can show no proof. It is also a good idea to leave copies of passports with friends or family at home so that in the event of loss, there is some proof of identity.

Ship's documentation
This is required by the Customs Officer at each port of entry. Check with the USCG National Vessel Documentation Center for the necessary documentation (see appendix 2). Boats without documentation risk fines or impounding.

Clearance from previous port
Arriving in a new country without valid clearance from the last port can cause problems, as is explaining why it took six weeks to sail from St. Lucia to Martinique (less than 30 miles). Illegal immigration and drugs are the things that upset the authorities when dealing with foreigners; don't give them cause to look at you more closely.

Cruising and fishing permits
These are not usually required though some islands (St. Lucia) will ask you where you intend cruising. Fishing permits are required in some islands; don't fish before checking on entry or you could upset local fishermen and officials.

Insurance and health certificate
An insurance certificate for the ship may be required if there is an incident involving a claim. Some marinas or boat yards may not admit an uninsured yacht.

Health certificates may be required if a crew member goes down with a complaint that might be covered by vaccination or inoculation.

Other certification
Carry bill of sale and tax papers as appropriate. Carry your dive certification when you have tanks refilled at a dive center or wish to hire gear and dive. They may not oblige otherwise.

Carry ship's radio license and operator's certificates as appropriate.

Finance

Currency

The official currency of most of the English-speaking islands is the Eastern Caribbean dollar or EC as it's known, whose price is fixed to the US dollar at around EC 2.67 (at the time of writing). The French islands of Martinique, Guadeloupe, St. Bart's (St. Barthelemy) and St. Martin use the Euro but readily take US dollars. The Netherlands Antilles, which includes Saba, Statia (St. Eustatia) and Sint Maarten (the Dutch side of St. Martin) quote prices in Dutch guilders but accept US dollars. Trinidad uses the TT dollar. The Virgin Islands (US and BVI) use the US dollar.

All the islands are strongly geared to tourism. The US dollar is the most widely accepted currency. Small traders will usually only accept cash in the local currency.

Make sure which dollar you are talking about before agreeing on a price for anything. It's too late at the end of a taxi tour to complain that you thought the fare was 25 EC$ (about 10 US$) when the taxi driver meant 25 US$.

Credit cards

Credit cards are accepted in every island by the larger shops, Visa and Master Card being the most popular. Some shops and boat yards make a surcharge for credit cards and you should ascertain the amount before doing business. American Express usually incurs a higher surcharge.

There are plenty of banks throughout the Caribbean and getting cash is not a problem as long as you have a recognized credit card and your pass-

---

Minding the store

Appointing an agent in the US to handle your various commitments while you are away will help to give you peace of mind that all's well back home. This agent can be a member of the family, a friend or professional agent. Whoever you choose will need to have authority to act on your behalf and may require a signed power of attorney to generally act in your interest. They may also need to pay bills and other accounts on your behalf, have access to funds and handle, sort and forward your mail. If you have property, rented or empty, it will need supervision. Elderly relatives in care or just getting older may need attention. All this is quite a responsibility to load on anyone's shoulders and the chosen person needs to understand your requirements thoroughly.

port. Most banks and some other places have ATMs (cash machines). Carry more than one credit card in case an ATM should eat your card (and they do sometimes for no good reason). If this happens you may be delayed in getting a replacement because the credit card company will usually only forward a new card to your billing address. If that address is in the US you must then arrange for the card's safe transport to wherever you are; not always the easiest thing.

There is a big trade in stolen credit cards and the Caribbean is no different from anywhere else. Guard your card. Keep the details in a separate place aboard.

Making money along the way

The possibility of financing your cruising budget by working in the Caribbean is a thorny subject. Except for U.S. citizens who enjoy all of their usual rights of citizenship in the USVI, you cannot just set yourself up in business and bank the proceeds in any of the islands without following local laws and regulations. Regardless of your trade or profession, selling yourself, your goods or services is against the law. That is not to say it doesn't happen, but moonlighting runs the risk of heavy fines or imprisonment plus confiscation of property, including your boat. Some islands, Trinidad for example, do not allow you to sell your goods or services even to another foreign-flagged vessel. "Swap, barter or trade" is allowed.

Selling your work outside the islands is permitted, thus you can be an off-shore consultant, writer, illustrator, yacht deliverer or any other work paid for outside the islands.

Chartering is another way of making money but you must have permission to charter your boat in the waters of the country in which you intend operating as there are fees and levies to be paid. Working the black market is risky and unfair to your host country. Having paying guests aboard requires your boat to have certain safety equipment and insurance and there is usually a per capita tax levied by the authorities of the country you're in.

If you have a particular skill or have professional qualifications that the island needs, you may be able to get temporary employment. This will involve considerable paperwork and time to secure a work permit and your employer will have to prove to the authorities that there is no resident islander who could fill the post. If you are sponsored by a local authority in the islands, then most of the required paperwork will be done by them on your behalf.

16

Security & insurance

To anyone unfamiliar with the Caribbean, what follows may give the impression that one takes appalling risks by sailing these waters. The truth is that, with appropriate behavior and some common sense, the Caribbean need be no more dangerous than life at home. It's just that the hazards are a little different and it pays to be cautious. Most cruisers spend years trolling up and down the island chain with no greater danger than running out of rum. Incidents, when they do happen (which is rare, given the ratio of crimes v cruisers) are so publicized that the real risks are blown out of proportion. Very often, as the facts emerge, it turns out that the incident might well have been avoided by a better appreciation of prevailing conditions and more appropriate behavior and precautions.

Security

Security of the boat, with regard to theft, piracy, illicit boarding by others is of concern to all cruisers, many of whom have put a good amount of money into their venture, with the boat itself being the largest chunk. Add to this the contents which seem to grow with each cruising year–every cruiser periodically raises the waterline–and you tot up a tidy sum.

It is a good idea to keep in radio contact with friends you meet along the way or cruise in company with another yacht in suspicious areas. Also keep some trusted person aware of your itinerary. Use caution before answering a call for help.

Lock it or lose it
Prudence is the watchword. Leave nothing loose outside the boat that you don't care to forfeit. Always lock the boat if you are leaving for more than a short while or after dark. Always lock up if leaving in the dinghy, unless you are within sight and easy reach. Trolling across the bay for a sundowner with another cruiser, you might not notice a departing dinghy loaded with

your goodies later on. Night falls quickly in the tropics. Boats have been burgled by cunning thieves who came and went from the far side while the owners were chatting on another boat not 100 yards away. Some spots are notorious. Close and lock all hatches when leaving the boat; it's tiresome, but better than being burglarized.

If you always lock the boat, it not only becomes an automatic routine but a clear indication when you return that your craft is intact. Cruisers we know did not realize they had lost passports, money and other valuables until several days after the event, by which time it was virtually impossible to discern when or where the theft had occurred.

This is not to suggest that every other cruiser is a dirty rat, far from it as 99.9 per cent of the cruisers you will ever meet will be the most honest, helpful and friendly people and most islanders, with their religious upbringing, are honest, but it is wise to be cautious.

Theft can happen anywhere. Always bear in mind that, to the average islander, you with your boat, no matter how modest, are a millionaire. It isn't fair to put temptation in anyone's way.

Don't carry your wallet in an open-top bag (women) or in your back pocket or backpack (men). In a jostling crowd it can be difficult to recognize an unintentional nudge from a sly assault with intent. Don't count your money in public if you've just been to the cash machine, don't pat the pocket containing your wallet to check its presence; miscreants watch for such indicators and may follow you. Carry only enough cash for the job in hand. These are no more than the precautions you would take at home.

Don't advertise your wealth by wearing gold jewelry. Leave your gold jewelry and gemstoned rings at home or in a safe place aboard. Fingers can and have been cut off for the rings they bore; the chopper won't stop to make a carat count to see if it's real. Islanders love to adorn themselves with gold, many have gold capped teeth and fingers weighted with rings. That's different. Admire, but don't emulate.

Tourists everywhere have always been fair game for villains; don't be an easy target. When ashore, and away from the marina environs, walk purposefully. Find out beforehand the No-Go areas of town and stay away. Walking alone is not always a good idea, take a buddy. Being aware of what's going on around you and giving an air of self-assurance will indicate to any potential pickpocket that you're in control so he'll choose an easier target. Before leaving the bank, having stowed your wallet in an inside pocket, glance outside to see who's still hanging around since you went in. The bad guys always go for the most unsuspecting victim.

Having said all this, however, there is no point in being paranoid about safety; the chances are that you're more likely to lose something overboard or down the bilge than forfeit your valuables to some crook. It's just a matter of being sensible to the different attitudes and conditions of your location.

Occupied yachts have been boarded by thieves, usually at night, and in some places—Venezuela in particular—it is a wise precaution to lock yourself below at night, leaving nothing of value in the cockpit or on deck.

The dinghy

As your dinghy is your primary means of getting to and from the mother ship, retaining possession of it is paramount. Dinghies are currency anywhere in the world and thieves will go to great lengths to relieve you of your craft or its equipment. Again, Lock It or Lose It. Equip the dinghy with a security line of heavy duty cable at least 16 feet long, with a swaged eye at each end. Padlock it onto an eye in the dinghy and pass it through the outboard handles and fuel container. When ashore, pass the free end of the cable through a suitable dock fixture and secure with a padlock. Chain works even better. The outboard should have an additional padlock through the securing bolt levers.

At night, hoist the dinghy with a bridle, at least to the toe rail taking the painter forward on the mother ship and secure it with chain and padlock. The nightly routine soon becomes second nature and as cruising dinghies spend a lot of time in the water, lifting also helps to slow fouling. A third benefit is that it stops the water chuckling and the dinghy nudging the stern during the night and disturbing your sleep.

Give your dinghy another name from the mother ship; 't/t Daffy Duck' only advertises your absence to those casing the dinghy dock. Thieves have been known to use the dinghy to board and burgle the mother ship, returning the dinghy to unload and make their getaway. Cheeky, but it happens.

Piracy

In the eastern Caribbean, piracy is of a very low order and in nearly ten years, we have heard of very few incidents involving foreign cruising boats. There have been some isolated acts of murder but again the circumstances have been unusual and in one case the alleged killer was a member of the crew.

Prudence is the watchword for cruisers. Don't advertise your (supposed) wealth. When on the radio, don't mention when you are going to be off your boat; the bad guys are taking notes. Keep your eyes open, your wallet closed and your boat locked.

Securing documents

Ship's papers, Customs and Immigration forms, and crew passports need a secure place aboard. Passports are currency. Keep a dedicated folder, preferably something substantial, waterproof and with a zip or good closure. This is one of the things to grab in the unlikely event of abandoning ship, as once ashore you'll need to prove your identity before anyone will help you. No matter how dire, dramatic and documented by the media the circumstances of your rescue might be, you are an illegal alien if you can't produce proof of your identity. Persuading your embassy that you are who you say you are, and to take you in, could be difficult as you stand there dripping in your tattered T-shirt, bleating that you've just survived 215 days on a raft with just crabs for company.

Guns

A number of US cruisers bring a gun aboard. Whether, in the event of a confrontation, the cruiser would be quick enough to unearth, load, aim and fire a sidearm with sufficient skill to wound or kill an assailant, before getting shot himself, having first discerned if the assailant was also armed, is debatable. What the sentence might be for a foreigner, up against a judge who is probably related to the accused, is also open to conjecture.

Most Customs regulations require you to declare all firearms carried on your vessel and these may have to be surrendered until you leave, somewhat negating their protective properties.

Drugs

Illegal drug dealing and abuse is a fact the world over and the Caribbean is only one of many waypoints for the trade. If you are clean you are unlikely to see much evidence of this vast and unsavory business. Most islands have zero tolerance when it comes to any of the mind-altering, hallucinatory, addictive and illegal drugs and the penalties are heavy with massive fines, imprisonment, confiscation of goods, including your boat.

Be very wary of taking anything from anybody you don't know and trust, particularly casual crew. As skipper, you are responsible for all crimes committed by your crew whether you know about it or not.

Insurance

There are no cheap options when it comes to insuring a cruising boat. The companies that specialize in marine insurance each have a slightly different slant with rates to match. For cruising in the Caribbean, underwriters make no distinction between the islands; none are beyond cover nor are any a "better bet" (though the area from the southern tip of Grenada down is considered out of the hurricane belt).

Most of the marine insurance companies limit the dates and zones for insurance cover. They will not cover damage caused by a named storm any time from 1 July to 31 October in an area bounded by 12°40'N to 35°N and 30°W to 100°W.

If you are planning to leave your boat in the Caribbean during the hurricane season, some companies will offer cover under special conditions. Sometimes partial cover (50% approx) can be arranged for boats remaining in the hurricane zone which, the company claims, is a strong incentive for the owner to take precautions in the event of an impending storm (why would we do otherwise?).

The islands are by no means empty of boats in the summer and most charter companies have punters all year except August. There are companies in the Caribbean, experienced with local conditions, who offer cover for the many boats who stay during the hurricane season. Search via the Internet. Generally, it is felt that hurricanes, being predictable these days with hi-tech satellite tracking, are an avoidable risk and therefore the number of boats at risk is small.

Trinidad is still the most popular place to spend the hurricane season, with Venezuela running second. The prudent cruisers in Trinidad will continue to monitor the systems coming off Africa as they can still bowl a low ball, with feeder winds pulling a hefty swell across the Gulf of Paria and causing havoc in Chaguaramas anchorages.

17

Health matters

Getting the right treatment

One of the questions often asked of cruisers is "What happens if you get ill?" The answer is much the same as at home. You self-medicate until you think you should see a doctor–then you find a doctor.

Don't forget the pharmacist. For minor ailments or just for advice, consult a pharmacist. The pharmacist can advise you on which over-the-counter medication might help (his training is nearly as long as a doctor's) or tell you if your condition requires a doctor. The pharmacist is up-to-date on all the latest medications and in many instances he can save you worry, time and money on whether to see a doctor or not.

Finding medical help

When you need to see a doctor the best course is to ask another cruiser in the anchorage, a pharmacist, or ask any local person to direct you to a doctor's office or consulting rooms. Martinique has one of the largest and best equipped hospitals in the islands.

Some marinas carry a list of physicians, dentists, vets etc, and if not, will probably be able to direct you to the nearest clinic or supply a phone number. The Safety and Security Net keeps a listing of hospitals, doctors, dentists, veterinarians and other practitioners throughout the island chain and can be contacted for details (see Chapter 18 for daily net schedules).

Most islands run an ambulance service and will attend road accidents; just be prepared for the media to get there first. Blood and gore get top ratings over politics and any incident will attract a crowd of curious onlookers. It's not unusual for the early evening news to carry close up shots of what's left of the body where it fell after a "chopping."

All cruise ships have doctors and medical facilities, though contacting them on the high seas via VHF may prove difficult. In the event of a medical emergency at sea calling 'Pan Pan Medico' on VHF channel 16 may bring help from any station listening. It is worth noting that the US Coast

Prevention is better than cure

Prophylactic treatment for malaria will be needed if you plan to travel more than 100 miles inland in Venezuela though it is not necessary in the Lesser Antilles. Make sure your tetanus shots are up to date and have the other shots you need well in advance as some require a top up after a short period. Your GP will advise what inoculations you need but they will probably include hepatitis A. You will need a certificate listing diseases covered, drugs administered, top-ups and dates. This is vital information for any doctor in a foreign country should you need treatment.

In 2000 there was a polio outbreak in the Dominican Republic and U.S. doctors were advising cruisers whose polio vaccinations were dated prior to the 1950s and 60s to get re-vaccinated. At the same time St. Vincent and the Grenadines were requiring polio vaccination certificates; these restrictions are likely to spread to other islands. Check with your doctor for your own coverage.

Dengue fever is endemic throughout the tropics and recent indications are that the disease is on the increase in the eastern Caribbean. It is another infectious viral disease transmitted by some aedes mosquitoes, seldom fatal but often very unpleasant; the after-effects can last for months. Symptoms include sudden fever, headache and acute pain in the joints. A second fever follows some days later with a rash. There is no preventive treatment but symptoms can be alleviated with painkillers, but *not* aspirin. Medical help should be sought. For the latest information on the current status re dengue and other diseases see the following website www.who.org (World Health Organization).

Don't go tramping through the jungle unless with a qualified guide and do not touch or pick up wildlife; snakes in particular can be deadly. Fruit bats are harmless but messy. In parts of Venezuela, the north coast and a few of the outer islands, vampire bats pose a real threat and you should secure all hatches and ports with adequate screening after dark. The bats bite without disturbing the sleeper and, having supped, will leave their victims to bleed copiously. Bug screening is sufficient to keep the bats at bay for netting sounds solid to a bat and they will not fight their way in.

In the event of a bite (by bat, rat, dog or other) you should seek immediate medical help as tetanus and rabies are a risk.

Ascertain your blood type and Rh factor and make a note of it. Keep all your medical information together in a sealable plastic bag labelled as such and in a safe place aboard. In the event of illness you may be *non compus mentis* and someone else will need to know where to find your medical history. It's a good idea to put a tiny Post-it note of your blood type with your passport.

Guard land stations do not have SSB radio facilities, relying on VHF and land lines (see Chapter 18).

The Caribbean sector covered by this book is well provided with medical services. Doctors train mainly in the US, Canada or Europe. Their clinics are usually well run and they have access to all the hospital services. All the routine operations are performed and you should have no fear of scattered chicken bones or chanting as a method of diagnosis or treatment. Charges are very reasonable compared with the US, waiting time short and many cruisers come to the Caribbean, and Trinidad in particular, for eye, hernia and other surgery. The BVIs are a cosmetic surgery mecca.

If you have medical insurance make sure it covers the areas and times you plan to cruise. Consult your local GP at home before you leave, explain what you intend doing and where and discuss what prophylactic measures you should take beforehand and what medications you should take with you. Have him check your records to see that you have the immunization required for the Caribbean and Venezuela. These are essential for diseases such as yellow fever which can be fatal and for which there is no cure. Ask for a "To Whom It May Concern" letter detailing your medical history and current condition and stating the generic term for any "prescription only" medication you may need to obtain while away.

Using the generic term is essential as the same drug from the same company may well have a different name in each country you go to. It's not unreasonable for a Caribbean doctor to refuse to prescribe a drug that you take regularly because he doesn't know your medical history and rattling your near empty bottle from the pharmacy back home may not convince him.

Before leaving the US, ask for a few antibiotics for the more common ailments plus a suggested list of over the counter medications for treating mild conditions. It is also worth asking for a supply of syringes and hypodermic needles in a couple of sizes suitable for intra-muscular injection. These come in sterile packs and, stored carefully, should ensure that if you find yourself in some backwoods area where you suspect the hygiene you can supply sterile equipment to the medic.

First aid

See that at least one member of the crew attends a first aid course before leaving. If you will be cruising short-handed, or with children, then it is advisable that both adults get certificated so that either can attend to boat or babe. Also, in a crisis, two heads are better than one. There are several good publications concerning first aid and major bookstores should be able to point you to the medical section where you can make your choice. Merck have an excellent *Nurses Manual*, easier to understand than the doctor's edition. Try the reference library to peruse books you think might be helpful to buy. Boat show book stands are a good source of marine related publications. *Your Offshore Doctor* by Dr Michael Beilan is aimed specifically at yachtsmen (see Further Reading) and worth having on board.

Safe storage of medicines

Dedicate a suitable locker as a first aid cabinet. Stock it with all your favorite patent medicines plus a good supply of any medication that requires a doctor's prescription. If you are going to be away for a year, ask your GP to prescribe enough for that period plus the letter mentioned above. Keep a selection of analgesics: aspirin, ibuprufen, as they have different qualities. It's worth paying the extra for enteric coated aspirin as it is less likely to irritate the stomach. There are some conditions (dengue fever) where aspirin should not be taken or by people with aspirin allergy or intolerance where any form of aspirin is contra indicated. Children under 12 should not take aspirin except on doctor's orders. Cold remedies, laxatives, indigestion aids and diarrhea treatments are all useful. Don't overstock as all these patent medicines are available throughout the islands.

A selection including sterile bandage packs, arm sling, eye patch, safety pins, cotton swabs, and sterile wipes should be stored in a suitable container. Specialized first aid boxes can be found but they can be expensive; you can make up your own with the recommendations of your local GP and pharmacist.

Audit and review the contents of your medical cabinet periodically for deterioration of items and check the expiration dates. The limits are set by law and are of the "fail safe" kind rated for storage under the worst conditions, heat, humidity, etc. It is best to get rid of unused antibiotics after the expiration date and get fresh supplies.

General precautions

Dehydration
One of the first things to guard against in the Caribbean is dehydration. You will be losing a lot of fluid through perspiration and you need to keep replacing it. Sweating results from exercise, fever, hot weather and stressful

situations. Adult beverages might also be consumed in greater quantities than at home; it's hard to resist the lure of a rum punch at the end of the day but you'll need the extra water to process it if you're not to end up with a thick head.

Diarrhea and vomiting quickly lead to dehydration; fluids and electrolytes must be replace immediately: 1 teaspoon of plain salt in 1 pint of water, with enough sugar to make it palatable, should be drunk slowly, to replace lost minerals. Sweating also loses salt which must be replaced through the diet. Muscle cramps are sometimes the result of insufficient salt in the system. Dehydration can cause headaches particularly after alcohol; before you reach for the pain killers try copious drafts of water.

The effects of dehydration are insidious. Not knowing when the next drink is coming, the body shuts down all systems to ensure enough fluid for the brain. Heat prostration can hit without warning, especially if you are out in the sun without a hat, pushing yourself too hard in the heat. Headache, dizziness, nausea and disorientation could indicate dehydration as do constipation, dry skin, aches and pains, headaches, swollen feet. Test your urine; it should be clear, pale yellow. Also pinch the skin on the back of your hand, it should snap back within one second. If not–drink more, at least half a gallon a day, and adjust to Island Time.

Water supplies

Domestic water supplies throughout the Caribbean are potable and you should have no qualms about tanking up. Babies and very young children should have boiled or pure bottled water as you would in the US. For drinking water treatment and filters, see Chapter 13.

Food hygiene

Water is a valuable commodity but spare none when washing fruit, vegetables and particularly salad. Some cruisers swear by potassium permanganate. Peel all fruit; you can also sear tomato and bell pepper skins over an open burner, otherwise, if it is to be eaten raw, a thorough wash should suffice.

Bacteria multiply fast in the hot humid conditions and garbage needs to be disposed of regularly. Keep work tops clear of debris and never leave food uncovered; microscopic flies seem to materialize out of nowhere. If you have a refrigerator, it will be working overtime and may not be able to keep sufficiently cool for perfect safety. Check the temperature regularly and reduce the time you usually expect to keep food fresh. Discard anything you're not sure about–it's better to waste a little food than risk an upset stomach.

Diswashing is another water-user but be sure to rinse detergent before draining items. Damp dishtowels harbor bacteria and it's better (and easier) to use very hot water and allow dishes to air dry then, if necessary, wipe the last remaining drips with paper towels before stowing away safely. Do the dishes as soon as possible rather then let them lie where they will attract flies and fester in the heat.

Dipping all fruit and vegetables bought in an open market, or even in a store, in sea water (in a large string bag) will help to flush out unwanted visitors if you suspect them. Dipping is also said to help bananas last longer. Keep all fruit and veggies below or you will attract fruit bats. They are harmless–just after a free meal–but they leave a horrid mess.

Body care

Skin

There can't be many people today who are unaware of the dangers of tropical sun on pale skin. There is no such thing as a "protective tan." A tan, though once considered attractive, is destructive and the damage is accumulative over time; no one wants to age faster than is strictly necessary. Skin is sun-sensitive, no matter how quickly it tans; the answer is to protect it. It's cooler, easier and more protective to wear baggy trousers or long skirts and long sleeved shirts and a wide brimmed hat. Sunscreen is death to varnish and a lot of other finishes, can stain fabric and leaves greasy marks over everything else. Sunscreen with a high factor is excellent on faces and backs of hands; don't forget tops of feet. Apply with a folded square of bathroom tissue and you won't get it over your palms and fingers. Look for sunscreen that protects against UVA (the ones that age you) as well as UVB (the rays that cause cancer). Drink plenty of water to keep skin plumped and young.

When in the sun wear a hat with a brim large enough to protect tops of ears and back of neck. Remember that, even in the shade, the sun's rays are reflected from the water, ground, deck and buildings. Even covered up you will still get enough of a tan to draw admiring comments on trips home.

Beware of cuts and bites for they can fester quickly in the moist heat. Do not cover small skin lesions. Clean with 10 per cent volume hydrogen peroxide (available at the pharmacy as a mouthwash or antiseptic) and keep dry but do not cover. At the first sign of infection (reddening and tenderness) apply antibiotic powder. If it hasn't cleared in two days or if there is a red trace up the limb and/or tenderness in groin, armpit or neck see a doctor. Blood poisoning and gangrene are not uncommon from a neglected, infected mosquito bite, as I discovered. Cactus plants abound on some islands and their small spines wait to spike the unprotected foot.

Don't swim with open wounds. Band-Aids (dressings) should be changed immediately if they get wet; a damp Band-Aid encourages festering. Lacking anything else, the skin of the papaya laid over a festering spot will cleanse it and ease itchy bites.

Ears

Ears need care in the tropics. Tops of ears need protection from the sun. After swimming and particularly after scuba or free diving, ears should be well rinsed with fresh water and a few drops of ear wash allowed to sit in the cavity. Ear wash can be made from 4 parts white vinegar to 1 part rubbing or isopropyl alcohol obtainable from pharmacies. Make up the mix and keep it in a small screw-top jar together with a small dropper obtainable from any pharmacy. Empty spice jars do well. Two drops in each ear after swimming will help to prevent ear infections which are common and can be quite painful, even damaging to your hearing. *Note:* Do not use isopropyl for camera or lens cleaning as, being denatured, it leaves a deposit.

Eyes

Eyes are sensitive to sunlight and optical quality sunglasses should be worn most of the time. The tropical sun reflects off all surfaces and the damage, as to the skin, is accumulative; also, squinting gives you wrinkles. Polaroid lenses afford a better view through the water to spot coral and shallows. People wearing glasses have the option of having their prescription lenses tinted or wearing clip-on sunlenses. The clip-on type that flip up are useful as they can stay on the glasses and be flipped up out of the way when going below or entering a building from the bright street.

Teeth

Dentists in the Caribbean, like doctors, are trained to US and European standards. You will find dental clinics in most islands. Ask at marinas, or other cruisers who frequent the area, for recommended practitioners. It is worth carrying a dental emergency kit, found in pharmacies, consisting of putty-like cement that can be used to fix a loose crown or replace a filling temporarily, until professional help can be obtained.

Feet

Feet come in for a lot of abuse aboard. There's always some piece of deck gear waiting to trap a toe or bruise a heel. Ideally, shoes should be worn

When cruising the Caribbean islands, it's not difficult to find a secluded bay all to yourselves – well almost.

whenever feet go on deck but this doesn't always work out and broken toes are not uncommon.

If you suspect you may have broken or cracked a bone in a toe, there is probably little point in seeking medical aid ashore unless there is a gaping wound that obviously needs stitching. In most cases the best treatment is to clean the foot and dry it well then strap the affected toe to its bigger neighbor as a splint. If the skin is grazed, sterilize with hydrogen peroxide. Keep the foot elevated, taking pain killers (ibuprofen) if necessary.

Watch for infection, particularly any reddening that extends upward from the foot, tenderness in the groin or pus from the wound. Bruising should show within 24 hours and fade gradually in the usual way but watch for any unusual discoloration. In most healthy people, bone heals quickly and the toe should be able to take light loads in 4–7 days and be nearly symptom free in 14. Additional vitamin C daily is said to aid healing in all cases. Suspected broken fingers can get the same treatment though strapping the digit in a finger splint (from the pharmacy) can help.

As with all self-medication treatments the rule is: If In Doubt, Seek Professional Help.

Other health hazards

AIDS

The disease is a health problem in most islands. The HIV virus, a precursor to AIDS, is primarily spread by the direct exchange of bodily fluids (sexual contact with an infected person and by drug abusers sharing needles). As mentioned earlier, a supply of syringes and hypodermic needles in sterile packs should be carried in your first aid supplies for use in the event that you require injections in less than perfect conditions.

Mosquito bites are not a risk as the virus cannot survive outside its living host so the biter cannot carry the virus from one person to another.

Mosquitoes and biting flies

Mosquitoes are not much of a problem aboard when anchored off; breezy anchorages are a deterrent and while malaria is rare in the Caribbean, mosquitoes can still be a pest ashore. Fresh blood is always welcome and dusk till dawn is mealtime. Cover up for sundowners in the cockpit in an enclosed anchorage or at the local beach bar, though mosquitoes have been known to bite through fabric.

Repellents are easy to obtain. Vitamin E taken over a period of time seems to make one less appetizing and less responsive and is also good for sun-damaged skin. Avoid scratching bites as they quickly become infected in tropical humidity. No-see-ums is the euphemistic name for microscopic flies whose bite is worse than a mosquito's and take longer to clear. The only resource is not to get bitten. They are more of a nuisance in the evenings and when walking in or near sand. Wear plenty of repellent and/or cover up. Treat bites with After Bite, a weak solution of household ammonia that works well to stop the itch.

Lighting mosquito coils and citronella candles in the cockpit helps. The fumes don't kill bugs but do seem to deter them.

Cockroaches

These pests are almost unavoidable but hardly a hazard; cockroaches are not harmful nor dirty and do not carry disease but most people find them repellent and they are destructive, chewing their way through most packaging to spoil the contents. Infestation tends to come aboard via corrugated cardboard boxes. The female lay eggs in the little tunnels. They also like the glue on can labels. When bringing stores back to the boat, offload all cardboard boxes in the dinghy or better still on the dock. Cockroaches are shy, preferring to forage at night and will scuttle away when the light comes on. If you spot one you may be sure there are 99 behind him. The female carries egg pouches but will drop them if threatened. Store all dry goods in hard plastic containers with airtight lids.

To prevent and treat infestation use boric acid powder, obtainable from the pharmacy. Sprinkle along the backs of all shelves in the galley or where food is stored. Pull out drawers and sprinkle behind them. Sprinkle in any crevices that look as if they might be a pathway: behind the stove, under the sink. The only thing to which cockroaches are susceptible is dehydration. The boric acid powder gets under the scales of their carapace and perforates the connecting membranes so the little beasts dry out. Do not mix the boric acid powder with sugar, honey or condensed milk; these only make a mess while not speeding the kill. Treatment takes about four weeks as one has to wait for the new hatchlings to emerge and paddle through the powder. Boat cockroaches are small and tan colored. Ashore you may find the 2-inch brown "mahogany mice" variety. There are all sorts of Roach Motels, sticky traps etc, but in our experience, nothing works as well as boric acid powder to make the ship a "cockroach-free zone."

Our two infestations both happened while hauled out for anti-fouling. The cockroaches, from a neighboring infested boat, climbed up the support struts and then up the hull. Subsequently, we did have some success wrapping sticky fly papers around the struts and the base of the ladder; this also deterred the ants. Many insects fly, including cockroaches, so vigilance is the watchword.

Ciguatera poisoning

This unpleasant condition is caused by eating affected fish. The poison is accumulated as it passes up the food chain so the biggest fish are the most heavily contaminated while remaining unaffected themselves. Only the reef predators are affected while pelagic fish are free of it. The northern end of the island chain seems to have more ciguatera than further south. To date, there is no reliable way of detecting an affected fish for it looks and tastes fine. The effects on humans usually appear within hours of eating the fish and, while pretty serious and painful, are seldom fatal. The symptoms include: vomiting, diarrhea and cramps. Tingling or burning of lips, tongue and extremities might also occur. If any of these symptoms are present after eating fish seek medical aid immediately.

Photo opposite: Energetic cruisers will take every opportunity to climb up an island hill to enjoy a tranquil bay and a scenic photo opportunity.

Rats

Yes, rats and other vermin have a place in paradise also. You are only likely to take on unwanted crew if you are at a dock for any length of time, where they can trot up the gang plank or jump or climb from the shore; rats can jump amazing distances. Stern lines to a tree can make a highway for anything that can cling and crawl, though wide disks threaded over the lines can sometimes deter all but the most acrobatic. If you are unlucky enough to get visited, don't bother borrowing someone's pet cat; most domestic felines are too smart to take on a rat and will give you that "You've got to be joking" look. Buy the rat and mouse traps available but be prepared to cope with the distasteful task of disposal. All vermin can carry disease, do not handle any creature, dead or alive. In the event of getting bitten, seek medical aid immediately.

Rats, mice (and some cats) just love chewing on electrical cables; this doesn't do a lot for the insulation nor for the culprit, if he gets his wires crossed.

Vegetation

The manchineel tree looks unremarkable but contact with the white sap will produce a painful skin rash and eating the aromatic fruit, which look like little green apples (Columbus called them death apples) can cause serious problems, sometimes fatal. The tree provides safe shade except in rain when the run-off from the leaves will also cause the rash. The tree grows along the roadside and some beaches though it has been removed from the more popular tourist beaches.

18

Communications

Keeping in touch with family and friends back home, and other cruisers afloat, plays a large part of life aboard and e-mail is one of the fastest-growing methods of communication for cruisers. Satellite telephones are good but expensive. Cell phones have limited use–see below. VHF and HF (SSB and Ham) radio are very popular as the air waves are free.

Mail

Mailing ordinary letters from most Caribbean countries is straightforward and many of the islands specialize in decorative stamps to attract collectors. Simple letters with no interesting contents usually reach their destination in 10–14 days. Incoming mail can present a problem in finding a reliable reception point. Marinas will usually accept mail for yachts in transit though they may have a time limit, after which the mail may be stored, returned or dumped. General delivery at the local post office is variable from island to island and not the preferred method by many. On some of the major islands specialist mail services will hold and forward mail for you at a charge. For bulk forwarding of mail to and from home, specialist mail services such as Fedex or DHL will be the fastest. Consult the cruising guides for suitable mail drops in your chosen island.

Anything more than flat mail coming in is likely to be stopped at Customs, who may send a notice to the addressee requesting collection. This could involve a trip to the Customs Office to open the package for inspection (expect a curious audience) and, if approved, its retrieval. If you need to receive an item by mail, make sure the appropriate Customs declaration is filled in by the sender.

Be aware that parcels may not arrive intact and even those sent by airmail can take more than a month to arrive. For boat parts or valuable items, the extra expense of using specialist mail shippers such as Fedex and DHL addressed to a reliable marina or shipping agent will give faster and safer delivery. Make sure the parcel is marked clearly with the yacht name and "For Yacht In Transit" to declare that they are not being imported.

In Trinidad, where many boats spend time for refit, all the major marinas and yacht clubs will keep mail for yachts and there has seldom been a problem receiving mail. Parts or equipment coming from outside Trinidad are not subject to import duty if they are for use on your boat. Check the latest regulations on arrival.

The storage of items at a post office, or awaiting collection, may not always be logical. The parcel for Arthur B Cruiser, Sailing Yacht *Great Spender* could be filed under any of the above capital letters and persuading the clerk to search under all names is an art.

Cellular phones

Most service providers in the Caribbean cover only a specific area and the phone may not work once out of it or there may be a hefty roaming fee. Each island, or area, usually requires a different number and one must register each time and then alert your friends with the new number, which is tiresome. If your lifestyle demands that you are in constant contact then these inconveniences are part of the price.

Satellite communication

Satellite telephones
Satellite telephones are for the seriously dedicated communicator and often essential for the person still running a business back home. The Inmarsat Mini-M service has proved reliable with voice and data (e-mail and Internet access) services available. The familiar white dome is definitely a prestige item. Satellites are expensive to build, launch and maintain, as a result this will not be the cheapest form of communication but for some will be the most convenient. Equipment and running costs are greater than other communication systems. Incoming calls are chargeable.

Satellite data communications—e-mail
Satellite e-mail using Inmarsat C is less expensive than Inmarsat Mini-M for text only and has also proved reliable. Being a satellite system, the same comments apply as for satellite telephones. Inmarsat C also provides a reliable method of receiving text weather forecasts. Messages in both directions must be sent as text only.

E-mail

E-mail onboard via SSB radio

Services such as SailMail and PinOak Digital provide text-only e-mail services over marine SSB radio. These services require a TNC (terminal node controller) or modem connected between your SSB radio and your onboard computer. The TNC available from and used by PinOak is only suitable for PinOak data communications. The SailMail system uses the same TNCs used by radio amateurs and is a viable option for radio amateurs also wanting to send and receive commercial traffic. The selection of a suitable SSB radio needs professional advice as some radios, such as the Icom IC-M710, are supplied with a suitable socket for connection to the TNC. Other radios, if suitable, might require internal wiring to make a connection. For further information on SailMail go to www.sailmail.com. For information on PinOak Digital go to www.pinoak.com. Cruise Email is a Florida based service which offers Caribbean service. For more information go to www.cruise.Email.com.

E-mail onboard via amateur radio

Ham radio can provide an inexpensive means of using e-mail on board. If you are prepared to qualify as an Amateur Radio Operator the option of free onboard e-mail is attractive. With a ham radio license and the hardware linked to his HF radio, an amateur can send and receive text-only e-mail even while under way. This works by the cruising ham signing on with a shore-based amateur radio operator who offers the service by linking to the Internet. Using the compatible software, messages can be sent and received almost as easily as ashore. The limitations are the prevailing atmospheric conditions or "connectivity" and, being amateur radio, no commercial transactions are allowed. So while you may e-mail your friend about a broken part you cannot order it via ham e-mail from the supplier. Nevertheless, friends and family can be kept up-to-date with your progress, plot your position and safe arrival even if they are not hams. The no-commerce rule of amateur radio operation means there is no charge for the service and the shore-based hams do it for free. The only cost to you is in the initial equipment, radio and modem, plus your amateur license. Hams using this service may also wish to take advantage of a service such as SailMail (see above) or Inmarsat C for commercial traffic.

E-mail ashore via cyber cafés

Many islands have cyber cafés where you can send e-mail. These services are one of the easiest and cheapest ways to keep up-to-date with your e-mail, contact suppliers or surf the web. Cyber cafés can be stand-alone offices with computers for rent on a timed basis or set up as part of a mail service business while others may be part of a shop or café. New outlets are springing up all the time as people realize the potential business to be had and the islands have been quick to respond.

Make sure that your e-mail address is easily accessible from the Internet without requiring any specialist software on your computer. At this time Hotmail and Yahoo addresses are the most popular. Some cyber cafés allow you to use your own disks to transfer text. Cyber cafés will provide the fastest available connections to the Internet as they are using the best local Internet Service Providers (ISPs). This is better than using your laptop with an international connection where data transfer rates may be very slow and the cost much greater. Typical cost (at the time of writing) of using a computer in a cyber café is US$2.00 to $5.00 for 15 minutes.

Laptop connected to local telephone

Some cyber cafés and people ashore with a land line telephone may allow you to connect your own laptop. ISPs (Internet Service Providers) such as AOL often have local telephone access numbers.

Laptop and acoustic couplers

This is now considered old technology and not practicable given unreliable telephone services. The current preference among cruisers is Pocketmail using public telephones–see below.

E-mail by public telephone using Pocketmail

Pocketmail combines keyboard, computer, modem and acoustic coupler in a unit the size of a pocket organizer. The Sharp TM-20 and Pocketmail Composer open like a case with a screen in the lid and keyboard in the base. Simple word processing allows writing and storing of messages plus addresses. Connection is made by dialing a special number and aligning the Pocketmail to the handset of any analog phone. Mail waiting to be sent is uploaded, incoming mail downloaded and a signal verifies a successful communication. In North America and the US Virgins, the call is free (800). Outside North America and from other islands, an international number is used. Using a telephone service provider for your connection is often quicker than a pay phone. As uploading and downloading of short text messages seldom takes more than one or two minutes the cost is bearable. Remind your senders to keep messages to text only and short. With a price of about $150, its loss overboard is not disastrous. The annual "all you can use" service charge is around $150 and we have used Pocketmail successfully between Europe and North America, including Canada and the Caribbean. For more information go to www.pocket.com/us/

Radio

Marine VHF, SSB and amateur radio are very popular in the Caribbean for inter-ship communication and listening to weather forecasts. Radio provides the means to keep in touch with other cruisers, particularly if they are buddy-boating or making a similar passage. Daily nets provide contact on SSB and VHF. SSB is increasingly used for data transmissions, such as weatherfax and e-mail. Amateur radio operators are very active in the Caribbean and often convey useful information even for the non-licensed listener. AM and FM broadcasts are also available for the listener looking for news and entertainment; VOA and BBC news programs can be received. Weather forecasts for the East Caribbean are broadcast by Navtex from Puerto Rico.

The US Coast Guard in Puerto Rico covers much of the Caribbean Sea but does not operate on SSB, relying on VHF and land lines. We have monitored SSB emergency traffic for a boat in difficulty nearing Panama being relayed to USCG in Miami–who cover that area–by cruisers near Carta-gena, Venezuela and a weather net operator in BVIs. The result was a happy ending but it does underline the advantage of carrying SSB radio. Emer-gency radio services also operate out of Martinique. See NP290 *Admiralty Maritime Communications*–Caribbean, UKHO.

VHF radio

For cruisers, VHF radio is still the most popular method of communication over short distances. On passage, Channel 16 is used as the hailing channel and, upon contact, another channel chosen for traffic. Strictly speaking, Channel 16 should only be used by vessels at sea but in the Caribbean you won't find a rigid adherence to this rule. Because of a lack of means of com-munication on many of the smaller islands in the past, VHF radio became established as the "phone line." As a result many of the services, such as laundry, diesel, water and ice, some of which come direct to your boat, can be contacted on VHF channels. Marinas and some restaurants will also take reservations via VHF and list their channels in the local cruising guides (see Chapter 9). Calling ahead to a marina is advisable if a berth is required, as places fill up quickly. In places such as Trinidad, where commercial traffic is heavy, VHF traffic is strictly for marine business.

On a security note, be aware that the world listens in on VHF and if you make a restaurant booking via this medium you can be sure that someone has made a note that you will be off your boat for the duration. Use something other than the boat name.

Because of the numerous US vessels in the Caribbean, many pleasure vessels in the Caribbean incorrectly use US VHF channels instead of in-ternational channels. In US territories US channels apply. Outside US territories, international channels apply unless otherwise directed. The same receive and transmit frequencies are used on the most important US and international VHF channels. Many of the international duplex chan-nels are used as simplex channels in the US and are designated with the letter A after the channel number. A list of the US Alpha channels follows.

Many US radios have both US and international channels. US VHF ra-dios also have weather radio channels to receive continuous weather broad-casts in the US, Puerto Rico and the US Virgin Islands. In the US Virgin Islands, NOAA continuous VHF weather broadcasts can be received on weather channel WX3 (162.475 MHz).

The following channels, which are international duplex channels, may be provided on US or Canadian VHF radios as simplex channels and desig-nated with the letter "A" as a suffix – 01A, 03A, 04A (Canada), 05A, 07A,

18A, 19A, 20A, 21A, 22A, 23A, 61A, 62A (Canada), 63A, 64A, 65A, 66A, 78A, 79A, 80A, 81A, 82A, 83A, 84A, 85A, 86A, 87A, 88A. Some radios may also have simplex channels 02A and 60A. Simplex channels 03A, 21A, 23A, 61A, 64A, 81A, 82A and 83A cannot lawfully be used by the general public in US waters. Channel 70 is to be used exclusively for digital selective calling for distress, safety and calling.

Anchorage VHF nets

In some anchorages where there is an almost permanent, though changing, population of cruisers you will find a daily net, usually in the morning, that gives information on local weather, events and a Help Wanted segment. Here, anyone needing information or help, be it the name of a good dentist or a refrigerator mechanic, can voice his request. These seldom go unanswered, as a busy anchorage is a hotbed of information and expertise.

Another popular segment of anchorage nets is the "swap, barter and trade" section. Cruisers are always adding to, replacing or repairing gear and the vital part or item may just be what another cruiser has two of or wants to be rid of. Items are offered on a "barterer beware" basis, but

The old fort at Marigot, St Martin.

there are many bargains to be had from the Treasures of the Bilge. Be aware that this bartering is only permitted between foreign-flagged vessels, as trading with local vessels or residents contravenes Customs regulations. In some islands, Trinidad in particular, items may not be sold for cash at all, even to another foreign vessel, so it is best to agree to terms privately, off the air.

The morning net reaches almost public broadcasting proportions in Chaguaramas, Trinidad during Carnival (held for a month ending on Shrove Tuesday) when the daily entertainment schedule is announced together with bussing arrangements for cruisers.

SSB Radio

SSB radio provides the necessary link for long distance (more than 20–30 miles) communication and many cruisers set up a schedule to keep in contact with friends as they move around the islands. This provides a nice touch to what can sometimes be a somewhat lonely lifestyle. Making friends is easy as cruisers are mostly like-minded. Differing itineraries, however, mean that saying goodbye happens more often than on land. With its greater coverage, SSB is an important tool in maintaining contact with friends while moving anchorages or making an ocean passage. There are many existing nets that you can join.

Many cruisers set up their own informal nets, on a time and frequency when they will listen, call and respond when conditions allow. There's no hard and fast rule about these nets, sometimes conditions aboard don't allow, or the crew are ashore or asleep. A net between two boats is referred to as a "sked." Some of the regular nets are listed below.

Contact frequencies are also used. Having made contact, boats move to another frequency; 6215 kHz is a popular calling frequency for boats wishing to make contact between 0700–0800. Other boats make contact on 8104 kHz before or after the Safety and Security Net. Before calling another vessel make sure that you have identified a clear frequency to move to.

US Coast Guard station NMN broadcasts regular daily weather forecasts for the Caribbean area on SSB frequencies. See the section on Sources of weather data in Chapter 11. Further details of SSB transmitting frequencies can be found in *NP281(2) Admiralty List of Radio Signals–Coast Radio Stations (Oceania and the Americas)*, UKHO.

Caribbean HF Radio Nets

The following is a list of some of the most popular nets. This list is not comprehensive and details of any further nets can easily be obtained locally.

UTC time	Local time	Frequency (kHz)	Mode	Net
1215	0815	8104	USB	Caribbean Safety & Security Net
1230	0830	8104	USB	Caribbean Weather Centre – David Jones
1300	0900	12362	USB	Caribbean Weather Centre – David Jones
1330	0930	16528	USB	Caribbean Weather Centre – David Jones

Public Correspondence
Public Correspondence stations are located in the US Virgin Islands, Virgin Islands Radio (WAH), and Trinidad, North Post (9YL). For further details refer to *Macmillan Reeds Nautical Almanac*, Caribbean edition.

FM and AM radio broadcasts
The Voice of America (VOA) and the BBC World Service can be received in the islands. Frequencies are subject to variations. Contact the broadcasters for free schedules and frequency information. Local FM stations broadcast music and local news and, in some cases, the weather.

Weatherfax
Weatherfax uses a dedicated unit or SSB or ham HF radio linked via a demodulator to a computer (laptop or desktop). Commercial software and demodulators are available and shareware and freeware for weatherfax reception can be downloaded off the Internet.

Navtex
Navtex weather forecasts for the Eastern Caribbean are broadcast by US Coast Guard station NMR in Puerto Rico, identification code [R].

Amateur radio (ham)
Amateur radio is a very useful means of communication and a good source of information. The Caribbean ham nets are very active and will be of interest even to the non-ham, who can listen in. The Caribbean Net, on 7241 LSB at 0700 to 0800 hrs local time is very popular. The Waterway Net, a group of mostly Florida-based ham radio operators, has many boating enthusiasts. For information about broadcoast schedules and membership, contact the officers via e-mail at WaterwayNet@aol.com.

In times of crisis, ham radio operators often provide the only communication link when hurricanes wipe out other means of contact on an island. Regularly, information on boats in a hurricane area has been provided via ham radio. Sending e-mail from onboard by HF radio, using a TNC modem with Pactor technology and an onboard computer has become very popular with hams. Connection through the Winlink network gives access to text weather forecasts, synoptic charts and other data in addition to the e-mail facility. Information is available on the Internet at www.winlink.org. 2m radio is also popular in some areas and several repeaters are accessible in the Caribbean. Find out the latest from local hams.

In some areas a reciprocal license may be required, but with the Universal License System now in effect you will be able to operate in a country that belongs to CEPT (EU countries) or with those that have signed the IARP agreement (Citel-Caribbean) without getting a reciprocal license. The AARL or Amateur Radio Caribbean net on 7241 kHz should be able to provide details.

Ham nets

The following is a list of some of the most popular ham nets. This list is not comprehensive and details of any further nets can easily be obtained locally in the Caribbean.

UTC time	Local time	Frequency (kHz)	Mode	Net
1035	0635	3815	LSB	Amateur Radio Caribbean Emergency Net (Jun 1-Dec 31)
1100	0700	7241	LSB	Amateur Radio Caribbean Net
1115	0715	7241	LSB	Amateur Radio Caribbean Weather
1125 (approx)	0725 (approx)	7086 +/-	LSB	Amateur Radio Caribbean Weather
1300	0900	21400	USB	Amateur Radio Atlantic Maritime Net
2030	1630	7086 +/-	LSB	Amateur Radio Cocktail Net

Radio etiquette

If you are in a busy anchorage or marina in the mornings when nets are active and you have made contact with another party on the net, try to choose a distant frequency from the net or band calling frequency for your traffic and keep your communication brief. Also try to avoid making data and un-necessary voice transmissions at the same time that the nets are running. Al-though the majority of your transmission will go out on the selected frequency, some of it may overpower the input stages of near-by stations using adjacent or other frequencies.

Other stations transmitting on HF close by can overpower your re-ceiver's input, resulting in interference on all channels preventing you from hearing a weak station. Usually tuning up and down the band will identify the station. Better to wait until that station has finished communicating be-fore transmitting as you may cause interference to other nearby listening stations. If possible, try to avoid transmitting on the same band when many other stations close by are listening to a net. If you must transmit, select a frequency as far as possible from other nearby stations. Make sure the fre-quency is clear. Never tune up on a frequency being used by anyone else. Tuning up on a nearby unoccupied frequency, plus or minus 6 kHz (at least) from the frequency in use, will normally give a good match to your antenna.

Plan to keep your conversation as brief as possible so as to give others a chance and remember that anyone may listen in.

Radio interference

Radio interference can be difficult to eliminate; you may need to switch other equipment off. Common culprits on board are refrigerators, inverters and battery chargers which cause interference on VHF transmissions, usu-ally a low frequency hum. On SSB reception, an inverter, some laptop com-puters and/or their small inverters, can cause interference on weak signals. Switch off the inverter or computer to see if this is the cause.

Transmitting on some HF frequencies can occasionally cause interfer-ence to electronics such as an autopilot. A different frequency may remove the problem. If you are experiencing problems you cannot resolve, get professional advice.

Beware of siting an active antenna, i.e., one supplied with 12V power to make it more effective, too close to any other active antenna. Electronics can interfere seriously with one another when running at the same time. Switching off one of the active antennas may help.

HF radio installation

Many visitors to the Caribbean experience difficulties with SSB radio trans-mission and reception. The biggest problem is usually the installation. HF radios, both marine and ham, must be properly installed to function cor-rectly. The power supply for the radio is normally the service battery bank and this must be able to supply a full voltage. Many marine and amateur radios are designed to operate from a voltage of 13.6V to 13.8V +/– 15 per cent. This operational voltage will only be met while charging the batteries from an alternator or generator. In practice, when an engine is not running, as will be the case with most sailboats, the radio will be operating from the lower range of its required input voltage. Special care needs to be taken to ensure that the wiring run from the batteries to the radio gives a minimal voltage drop; preferably less than 3 per cent.

The voltage on charged batteries may drop, when other loads are drawn, to below 12.0 volts. This is getting very close to the bottom end of the required input voltage. When you transmit under these circumstances, the voltage drops further and your transmission may go out distorted and often unintelligible to the recipient. Make sure that you keep your batteries well charged and that the radio is professionally installed to minimize voltage losses from the power supply.

For a good radio installation, the next two areas of importance are the connection to the antenna and the antenna ground. The radio must be positioned in a dry, well ventilated area, because some of the energy from the transmitter is radiated as heat. The radio should have an automatic antenna tuner fitted to the output. A manual tuner can be used to match the transmitter output to the aerial, but in practice, with the need to change frequencies or channels often, a manual tuner is not practical.

The antenna tuner should be as close as possible to the exit point, within the boat, of the feeder wire to the aerial. The feeder wire must be of the correct type and of minimal length to an insulated backstay or other part of insulated rigging. To ensure the maximum signal, a good antenna ground is essential. Unless you have considerable understanding of marine electronics seek professional advice when installing an SSB radio.

Safety and licensing

For maps and details of areas of responsibility for maritime safety in the Caribbean, see *NP290 Admiralty Maritime Communications–Caribbean*, UKHO. Boats traveling out of US waters are well advised to get a license. Specifically two licenses are required to use international VHF channels and SSB channels. A "Ship's Station" license is given to the primary radio of the vessel. A Restricted Radio Operator Permit (RROP) is technically required of each person on board who might use the radio.

19

Cruising couples

How to cope with cruising

In the cruising world, cruisers tend to be couples, with, or more often without, children and many of these seawives are also keen sailors.

The reluctant seawife

Some women, however, are cruising in order to be with their partners, suffering the discomforts of seasickness, disinclination or fear that afflict more women then men; others are reluctant to even think of cruising far from home. Maybe it's because women are, by nature, the bearers and carers that they see more dangers, real or perceived and this plays a part in affecting tolerance of motion and risk.

All research (including by such august bodies as NASA and GlaxoSmithKline) shows that women are much more susceptible to motion sickness, even before the age of 3 and suffer more from post-anesthetic nausea.

Furthermore, there is an enzyme in the brain, called MAO (monoamine oxidase), the amount of which determines the inclination to take risks. The less MAO, the more likely you are to take risks, while more MAO inhibits the desire to take risks. Generally, women have more MAO than men and we all have more as we grow older. This partly explains why young men are more likely to want to live fast and dangerously while girls are a little more wary, and all of us get more cautious with age.

Men have a *left brain* bias giving them a proclivity for logical thinking. This also results in them being less emotionally aware and/or less affected. They are also less sensitive to input stimuli, including internal bodily clues. Women's *right brain* makes them more emotional and more sensitive to internal and external clues. It also helps them to combine a lot of different talents into dealing efficiently with simultaneous multi-facet situations; they score well on fine detail tasks.

People with a passion for something sometimes find it difficult to accept that others may not appreciate or share their enthusiasm to the same

The critical list

If the thought of your partner's long term cruising plans is filling you with gloom or even if you are just a little dubious about the whole project, there are various things you should consider. First, it is a good idea to list on paper all your reservations, prioritizing if possible and leaving space for comments; it's a great help to see things on paper. Then list all the requirements you think might make life aboard more appealing and comfortable for you. This may include things apart from boat equipment, such as a periodic flight home.

Have an open discussion, with all points taken one by one. See if there is a solution or way around each problem and list it. For instance, your biggest fear might be seasickness.

- What can you do about it?
- What medications work best for you?
- Do you eventually get your sea legs?
- Are you prepared to tolerate life until that happens?
- Can you be excused of all duties while feeling miserable?
- Can the cruising itinerary be planned in the least arduous way?
- Can someone take your place for passage-making while you travel to the cruising ground by more acceptable means?

degree. If they have never felt sick or nervous on a boat, another person's misery might be dismissed as weak-minded or "it'll be better next time." It isn't and it won't be.

Whatever the reason for the reluctance, any cruising seawife who thinks she is the only one sacrificing herself to her partner's passion for sailing should take comfort that there are plenty like her out there. For this topic we will assume that the man is the enthusiast and the woman is reluctant, for whatever reasons.

Compromise

There is no merit in martyrdom and if one member of a partnership wants to cruise and the other is reluctant, the two should either part company for the duration or make some sort of compromise that allows them to be together for the best bits while the enthusiast does the rest. A woman should feel no compunction because of her natural reluctance to leave dry land, nor should she feel any compulsion to suffer unduly just because her partner wants to cruise.

There are so many combinations that can ease or resolve the situation for both sides. Obviously, some solutions cost money but if it means that the woman can accept and enjoy the cruising when she might otherwise remain at home, or they don't cruise at all, then it should be considered.

An agreement to try it for a year and then reassess the situation gives you the chance to opt out if life really is intolerable, without having to commit for an indefinite period. Many women like the security of a plan or schedule, even if it has to be modified along the way; the thought of unstructured wandering may sound romantic to a man but some women find it unsettling. If amicable compromises can be made on both sides without either party being guilt-ridden then happy cruising is almost guaranteed.

Getting there—and back

Getting the boat to the cruising ground can be done by having friends to crew or booking crew through an agency. The owner can engage a delivery skipper while he and his partner fly out. Buying a suitable boat in the desired cruising area does away with long sea passages (see Chapter 4). The boat can be kept in a preferred cruising area, storing it there in the off season or when both parties want to spend time at home. Limiting the cruising ground limits the passage-making.

With the initial long passage taken care of, adopting a routine of day hops with plenty of lay days in between can raise the acceptance level. This is the practice of most cruisers who can spend weeks in one place. Even so, some men like to push the boat as fast as she will go, even if they are only making a two-hour passage but their partners might find it more tolerable if sheets are eased, the boat less pressed and the motion improved. Not setting too vigorous a schedule can go a long way towards improving onboard moral. There is very little resemblance between sailing in chilly New England waters and cruising in the Caribbean where life is slow and easy. What's the big rush? Adjust to Island Time.

Another big reservation for women is being parted from family and friends; many women find it hard to sail away into the sunset with no plans to see kinfolk again in the near future. Finding some workable plan that allows the woman to keep contact or go back and hug her folks periodically can help. It is a gender thing; it's mostly the women who pine to go home and the men who are unfazed.

Some places in the Caribbean offer inexpensive fares. With the Internet accessible at cyber cafés throughout the islands, bargain fares may be found and plans made around the best dates. The lack of communication with family back home is high on most women's list. The advent of easy e-mail has made a great difference to cruisers, particularly with international phone calls being expensive, snail mail being slow and both services unreliable.

Home comforts

Primitive conditions aboard are sometimes raised as objections to cruising. After living in a spacious modern house with an all-electric kitchen, proper plumbing, a deep bath, washing machine, unlimited hot water, telephone and a car to go to town, life can look a little bleak when contemplated without them, plus the cramped quarters on a wobbly platform. What concessions to home comforts can be made in the boat to make it more comfortable? For myself, a real shower made a big improvement to my comfort, plus a proper bed where I didn't have to drop the saloon table nor climb over my pillows to get into a coffin. A refrigerator makes catering easier.

A fast, dry and stable dinghy provides speedy transportation without getting drenched in salt water. Both partners being involved with some of the boat handling helps to boost confidence. Women are good at detail and some seawives find an unexpected skill for navigation. Radio is another area where women excel and small skills build confidence.

When anchoring, agree on a well-rehearsed signal system to forestall that embarrassing rise in decibels or the measured tones of ill-concealed irritation. Women are often better at the helm and knowing your place in the scheme of things helps to avoid those demoralizing episodes we all dread.

Esthetics aboard, or lack thereof, is another reproach but nowhere does it state that ships must be Spartan, without any comfort. See where and how you can make the boat more homelike below. Attractive loose covers in your favorite colors will brighten the saloon and, being washable, will help to keep the boat pleasant. Silk flowers can replace the real thing. A large picture frame on the bulkhead filled with a collage of family photographs helps to keep dear faces familiar. Attractive bed linen and scatter cushions make a bunk more like a bed. Rubber-backed mats in toning colors make the floor less like a barrack, creating a homey look. They are non-skid, help trap the dust, can be shaken overboard, laundered when necessary and are nice underfoot.

Bring whatever personal things spell home. If you like crafts or have hobbies, bring them with you; a small sewing machine is invaluable. Sketching and painting the local scene is a nice way to keep a pictorial account of your travels; pack your gear. Anyone with musical talent can be assured of a welcome everywhere, bring your instrument; we've seen an upright piano in one cruising boat, a violin and many with guitars– impromptu concerts are popular. Musicians can play for their supper in many places.

Photo opposite: *Our boat* Honey Jar *lies quietly, stern to the shore, in Little Harbour, Peter Island, BVI. It was here, sitting in the cockpit, that I wrote a good deal of this chapter.*

Favorite islands

If I were asked to nominate my favorite cruising ground for the beginner I would unhesitatingly suggest the British Virgin Islands; they are exceptionally beautiful and must surely seduce even the most reluctant cruiser. The many islands, with their peaked and rolling green hills, lie barely a mile or two from each other, all offering a choice of safe and pretty anchorages, good walking, turquoise water, superb swimming and snorkeling plus palm-shaded white beaches and a cooling breeze. The views are mostly over to other islands, there are no open seas or overnight passages and if escape is essential, there are daily flights from Tortola.

Yet civilization is still here when needed, the postal system works better than down island, you can get all you need from the variety of stores and tourist shops. You'll soon have a circle of cruising friends who will offer a type and strength of friendship and support not often found ashore. For further encouragement read *Cruising for Cowards* and *Cruising in Comfort* by Lisa Copeland who, despite seasickness, made a circumnavigation with her husband and three young sons (see Further Reading for details).

Don't pass up the opportunity to experience this very different and enriching way of life. Give paradise a go.

20

Where next?

As June draws near, you need to think about where you and/or your boat are going to be for the hurricane season. Many cruisers stay in the Caribbean all year round and the charter companies only stop in August for maintenance. If you want to be out of the hurricane belt you should start considering your options early, depending on your chosen direction.

Checking your options

Insurance companies consider the southern end of Grenada below the hurricane belt and there is a thriving cruising community all year round.

Trinidad is a strong favorite where many cruisers haul and re-fit or store and fly home; there is much to occupy the cruiser other than sailing. The summer (hurricane season) is very hot with almost daily torrential rain making outside jobs such as repainting something of a gamble.

Going south east from Trinidad, the Orinoco River, Guyana, Surinam and the Amazon River make interesting cruising though you may be doing a lot of motoring as the winds can be light and fickle.

Going west from Trinidad, Venezuela is popular, being so close and downwind. Puerto la Cruz has several boat yards but not all the workers speak English. There are many interesting inland tours; Canaima and the spectacular Angel Falls being tops. There is enjoyable cruising, especially in the out islands. There is more crime near the bigger towns but plenty of cruisers enjoy a safe season; check among those who have been there most recently.

The Dutch Antilles, Aruba, Bonaire and Curaçao lie roughly 40 miles apart and 40 north of the Venezuelan coast. Though dry and arid ashore, Bonaire boasts some of the best underwater scenery in the world for divers.

If you are planning to go through Panama, your Caribbean cruising will have to be short as you should be in the Colón area by February or March,

There are many options for escaping the hurricane belt. Bermuda sits like the hub of a great wheel and makes a popular staging post for many cruisers.

which seems a pity if you only arrived at Christmas. Cartagena is a waypoint to Panama with the San Blas islands as an interesting time filler.

Continuing clockwise, Rio Dulce in Guatemala, is another option. Once through the shallows at the mouth of the river, the cruising beyond is gentle, through beautiful scenery. The recent floods may have destroyed some of this area. Check for recent news and local knowledge.

Going north to the US East Coast, you can track through Puerto Rico, the Dominican Republic and the Bahamas which are all nice but you need to be leaving the Abacos by early May if you are to clear Florida and 32°N, for insurance purposes, by June 1. Even then, hurricanes have a nasty habit of swiping the lower southern states.

If you are interested in exploring the East Coast, then you might look at entering the Intracoastal Waterway (ICW) somewhere in Florida and working your way up through the southern states. The ICW runs all the way up to the Chesapeake Bay. Wetlands border the East Coast, riddled with serpentine channels and rivers winding their way through reed beds, sand dunes and woodland. In some places the channel is across large sounds where the low shores are barely visible, giving the impression of being at sea. The ICW is a busy highway for those going south in the winter and north in the summer; joining the snowbirds gives you the chance to explore many of the historic places that you may only remember from school. After that you can spend the summer in the Chesapeake Bay or make a beeline for New England and the Canadian Maritimes.

Bermuda

Bermuda sits like the hub of a huge wheel with the Caribbean, Beaufort, North Carolina, New York, Maine and Nova Scotia all within a 6- to 7-day passage and the Azores about 10 days. Bermuda is a charming set of seven main islands, where the culture is staunchly British. Stopping here for a while to break the journey makes wintering in the Caribbean and summering in New England or the Canadian Maritimes an easy possibility as we found for five years running.

Weather net for Northern Atlantic cruisers

Herb Hilgenberg, a name familiar to many cruisers, has been running a weather net covering the North Atlantic for many years, originally from Bermuda but now operating from Canada as station VAX498, South Bound II.

Herb's knowledge of Atlantic weather patterns is legendary and he has an almost uncanny ability when it comes to forecasting. His daily net, starting at 1600 AST (2000 UTC) on 12359 kHz, can last for more than three hours and cruisers on his list check in with their location, local weather conditions and their intended routes. Herb then gives them a personal forecast on what they might expect together with abundant advice on tactics. His help, which is free, has been invaluable to many cruisers over the years and has been instrumental in search and rescue situations. Many cruisers won't put to sea until they've spoken to Herb. Check in up to 20 minutes before the start of his net. Many cruisers do not log in with Herb but listen to his forecasts for their area. It is also a way of keeping up with another cruiser's progress. Visit Herb's site at www.hometown.aol.com/hehilgen/

21

Some Caribbean Terms

Here are some uniquely Caribbean words and phrases as well as some specific Carnival terms.

Caribbean Terms

Some Caribbean terms and their explanations

Bacchanal	The uninhibited spirit of Carnival, the free-for-all fun and excitement of the feast
Chip	To follow a street band, shuffling along in time to the music without lifting your feet
Dingolay	A sinuous body movement down to the ground, similar to limbo—only for the young and fit, without a back problem
Fete	A party
Grind	Dancing by grinding your body against your partner's to the appeal of both. See also Dingolay, Jammin', Wine
Irie	Euphoric state of mind, because you are at a Jump Up (qv) in love, intoxicated or under other influence
Jammin'	An advance on grinding (qv) and wine (qv). Dancing with a little more graphic animation of the pelvis
Jump Up	A party, dancing, loud music, plenty alcohol and heaven knows what else
Limin'	Standing around with your friends, just passing the time of day. The boys watch the girls and vice versa
Pan	A musical instrument made from the tops of oil drums requiring an exceptional degree of skill to play. Erroneously called steel drums by foreigners
Wine	To gyrate the lower body around and around in an interesting fashion. Practice from childhood engenders a most remarkable mobility of the lower torso that is quite fascinating to watch

Specific Carnival terms

Calypso	A song whose clever lyrics can be funny or sad and often make a political statement, expressing discontent with the establishment or poking fun at public figures. The original means for the oppressed to vent their opinions
Calypso tent	A venue for variety shows with singers, dancers and comedians. Very funny once you tune your ear to the local accent and are abreast of current affairs
Soca	A mix of soul and Calypso; a modern combination of new and old music
Dimanche Gras	The top show to judge the Calypso Monarch and the King and Queen of the Bands, held on Carnival Sunday
Dirty Mas	The darker side of Carnival, where revelers carouse in the early hours of J'Ouvert (qv)covering themselves and others with mud and oil
J'Ouvert	Pronounced 'Joo-vay'. The 2 a.m. start of Carnival Monday
Mas	Short for masquerade, to dress up in costume, the parade of the bands
Mas Camp	Where the costumes are made for a particular band. Visit various camps to see the extraordinary diversity and ingenuity that goes into the costumes
Parang	Christmas music with a Latin American flavor and sung in Spanish
Pretty Mas	Costumed parades held during the day of Carnival Monday and Tuesday

Some traditional Carnival characters

Jab Jab	A devilish individual with horns and a tail and usually covered in black grease
Jab Molassie	Equally devilish but covered with molasses
Midnight Robber	Wearing a big black hat with a bigger, blacker attitude and an even bigger mouth he challenges his adversaries to a war of words
Pierrot Grenade	The robber's enemy, he takes his costume inspiration from Harlequin
Moko Jumbies	Wearing unbelievably tall stilts, these towering characters in colorful costumes dance and prance through the crowds

Appendix 1

Further Reading

The Boat and maintenance

Boat Ower's Mechanical & Electrical Manual, Nigel Calder, International
   Marine
Marine Electrical and Electronics Bible, John C. Payne, Sheridan House
Modern Boat Maintenance, Bo Streiffert, Sheridan House
Refrigeration for Pleasure Boats, Nigel Calder, International Marine
Understanding Boat Batteries and Battery Charging, John C. Payne,
   Sheridan House
Used Boat Notebook, John Kretschmer, Sheridan House

Navigation, weather and communications

Caribbean Yachting Charts, Nautical Charts, GmbH, Arnis
Celestial Navigation in a Nutshell, Hewitt Schlereth, Sheridan House
Concise Guide to Caribbean Weather, David Jones, The Caribbean
   Weather Center
NP7A, Admiralty Sailing Directions, South American Pilot, Vol. IV, UK
   Hydrographic Office
*NP71, Admiralty Sailing Directions, West Indies Pilot (North Western
   Part), Vol. II*, UK Hydrographic Office
*NP 281(2 Admiralty List of Radio Signals–Coast Radio Stations
   (Oceania and the Americas)* , UK Hydrographic Office
*NP283(2), Admiralty List of Radio Signals–Maritime Safety Information
   Services (Oceania and the Americas)* , UK Hydrographic Office
NP290, AdmiraltyMaritime Communications–Caribbean, UK
   Hydrographic Office
Reed's Nautical Almanac, Caribbean Edition, Thomas Reed Publications
Sailor's Weather Guide, 2E, Jeff Markell, Sheridan House

Cruising

Chance the Tide, Kenneth Mowbray, Sheridan House
Cruising for Cowards, Liza Copeland, Romany Publishing, Canada

Comfortable Cruising, Liza Copeland, Romany Publishing, Canada
Cruising with Children, Gwenda Cornell, Adlard Coles Nautical and
    Sheridan House
Handbook of Offshore Cruising, 2E, Jim Howard, Sheridan House
Ready for Sea! Tor Pinney, Sheridan House
Sell Up and Sail, Bill & Laurel Cooper, Adlard Coles Nautical and
    Sheridan House
The Voyager's Handbook: The Essential Guide to Blue Water Cruising,
    Beth Leonard, International Marine

Cruising guides
Cruising Guide to the Leeward Islands, Chris Doyle, Cruising Guide
    Publications
Cruising Guide to the Virgin Islands & Eastern Puerto Rico, Nancy &
    Simon Scott, Cruising Guide Publications
Cruising Guide to Trinidad & Tobago, Chris Doyle, Cruising Guide
    Publications
*The Gentleman's Guide to Passages South: The Thornless Path to
    Windwad*, Bruce Van Sant, Cruising Guide Publications
Sailor's Guide to the Windward Islands, Chris Doyle, Cruising Guide
    Publications
Virgin Anchorages, Nancy & Simon Scott, Cruising Guide Publications
World Cruising Routes, Jimmy Cornell, Adlard Coles Nautical
Yachtsmans' Guide: Virgin Islands, Eastern Puerto Rico, Meredith Fields

Health
Merck Manual of Medical Information – Home Edition.
Your Offshore Doctor, Dr Michael Beilan, Sheridan House

General
Caribbean Cookery, Best of Barbados, Jill Walker
Kitchen Afloat, Joy Smith, Sheridan House
Reluctant Cook, Jane Gibb, Adlard Coles Nautical

Appendix 2

Useful addresses and Websites

Cruising Associations

Seven Seas Cruising Association
1525 South Andrews Avenue, Suite 217,
Ft Lauderdale, FL 33316

Tel: 1 954 463-2431 *Fax*: 1 954 463-7183
Internet: www.ssca.org
E-mail: membership@ssca.org

Royal Yachting Association
RYA House, Romsey Road,
Eastleigh, Hampshire SO50 9YA
United Kingdom

Tel: +44 (0) 23 8062 7400 *Fax*: +44 (0) 23 8062 9924
Internet: www.rya.org.uk

Yacht transport

Dockwise Yacht Transport, (USA) Inc,
1535 SE 17th Street, Suite 200,
Ft Lauderdale, FL 33316

Tel: 1 954 525 8707 *Fax*: 1 954 525 8711
Internet: www.yacht-transport.com

Charts and publications

Sheridan House Inc.
145 Palisade Street
Dobbs Ferry, NY 10522

Tel: 1 914 693-2410 *Fax*: 1 914 693-0776
Internet: www.sheridanhouse.com
E-mail: sheribks@aol.com

Tides End Ltd
Bellingham Chart Printers,
PO Box 1728,
Friday Harbor, WA 98250

Tel: 1 360 468-3900 *Fax*: 1 360 468-3939
Internet: www.tidesend.com
E-mail: sales@tidesend.com

Bluewater Books & Charts
1481 SE 17th Street Causeway
Fort Lauderdale, FL 33316

Tel: 1 954 763-6533 *Fax*: 1 954 522-2278
Internet: www.bluewaterweb.com
E-mail: help@bluewaterweb.com

Imray, Laurie, Norie & Wilson Lt

Internet: www.imray.com

Caribbean Compass
Brick House
Back Road
Bequia
St Vincent and the Grenadines

Internet: www.caribbeancompass.com

Radio and weather

American Radio Relay League (ARRL)
225 Main Street
Newington, CT 06111

Tel:1 860 594 0200
Internet: www.arrl.org/
E-mail: tis@arrl.org

Federal Communications Commission (FCC)
445 12th Street, SW
Washington, DC 20554

Tel:1 888 225 5322 (1 888 CALL FCC)
Internet: www.fcc.gov/

The Caribbean Weather Center Ltd
Columbus Centre,
PO Box 3069,
Road Town, Tortola,
BVI, West Indies

Tel: 1-284-494-7559 *Fax*: 1-284-494-5358
Internet: www.caribwx.com
E-mail: weather@caribwx.com

Herb Hilgenberg,
South Bound II, VAX498

Internet: www.hometown.aol.com/hehilgen/
E-mail: hehilgen@aol.com

The Caribbean Maritime Mobile Net

Internet: www.viaccess.net/~kv4jc/

Health

World Health Organization

Internet: www.who.com

Caribbean yacht brokers and charters

Southern Trades
Tortola
British Virgin Islands, West Indies

Internet: www.southerntrades.com

Yachtworld

Internet: www.yachtworld.com

Bay Island Yachts

Internet: www.bayislandyachts.com

The Moorings
19345 US Highway 19N, 4th Fl.
Clearwater, FL 323764

Tel: 1 888 703-3176 *Fax*: 727 530-9747
Internet: www.moorings.com

Sunsail USA
Annapolis Landing Marina
980 Awald Drive, Suite 302
Annapolis, MD 21403

Tel: 1 800 735-4952, 1 410 280 2553
Internet: www.sunsail.com

TMM 1-800-633-0155

www.sailtmm.com

General

Boaters' Enterprise Ltd.
Cruise Inn Marina Village Square
Chaguaramas
Trinidad, West Indies

Tel: 1 868 6342055 *Fax*: 1 868 6342056
Internet: www.boatersenterprise.com
E-mail: boaters@trinidad.net

USCG National Vessel Documentation Center
792 T J Jackson Drive
Falling Waters, WV 25419

Tel: 1 304 271 2400 *Fax*: 1 304 271 2405

Index